W9-CMI-222

LANDSCAPE QUILTS

Nancy Zieman and Natalie Sewell

*To Pat —
enjoy!
Natalie Sewell*

OXMOOR HOUSE®

Landscape Quilts
by Nancy Zieman and Natalie Sewell
from the "Sewing with Nancy" series
©2001 by Nancy Zieman, Natalie Sewell, and Oxmoor House, Inc.
Book Division of Southern Progress Corporation
2100 Lakeshore Drive, Birmingham, Alabama 35209

Published by Oxmoor House, Inc., and Leisure Arts, Inc.

Library of Congress Catalog Number: 2001-132653
Hardcover ISBN: 0-8487-2470-4
Softcover ISBN: 0-8487-2483-6
Printed in the United States of America
First Printing 2001

Editor-in-Chief: Nancy Fitzpatrick Wyatt
Senior Crafts Editor: Susan Ramey Cleveland
Senior Editor, Editorial Services: Olivia Kindig Wells
Art Director: Cynthia R. Cooper

Landscape Quilts
Editor: Rhonda Richards
Copy Editor: L. Amanda Owens
Editorial Assistant: Suzanne Powell
Associate Art Director: Cynthia R. Cooper
Senior Designer: Emily Albright Parrish
Director, Production and Distribution: Phillip Lee
Associate Production Manager: Larry Hunter
Senior Photographer: Jim Bathie
Photographer: Brit Huckabay
Illustrator: Kelly Davis

Contributors
Photographers: Dale Hall, Keith Harrelson
Photo Assistant: Bill Freeman
Makeup Artist: Dell Ashley
Proofreader: Laura Morris Edwards
Illustrator: Laure Noe

We're Here for You!
We at Oxmoor House are dedicated to serving you with reliable informa-
tion that expands your imagination and enriches your life. We welcome
your comments and suggestions. Please write us at:
Oxmoor House, Inc.
Editor, *Landscape Quilts*
2100 Lakeshore Drive
Birmingham, AL 35209

To order additional publications, call 1-800-633-4910.

For more books to enrich your life, visit **www.oxmoorhouse.com**

Thanks to Heart to Heart Quilt Shop and Sew Bizz in Trussville, Alabama,
for use of their shops and Pfaff sewing machines for photography.

Seeds for this book began to grow more than three years ago when the two of us shared landscape quilting techniques on a Wisconsin Public Television program called *Wisconsin Quilts.* That PBS segment was followed by two three-part television series, the first on trees and the second on flowers. Then came this book, into which we have poured everything we ever discovered—separately and together—about how to make landscape quilts.

What makes this technique unusual, we think, is its freedom, its spontaneity. You don't have to plan ahead. You don't have to draw your scene in advance. You make no templates and cut no patterns. Unless you're making a fence or a structure, you don't even have to measure anything (until you get to the border). All you do is cut up fabric and glue it to a background fabric to make a favorite scene.

Of course, along the way, we learned from our own successes and failures. We learned how to cut for distant scenes and how to cut for close-ups. We learned how to glue—and how not to glue. We learned to look at fabric in a whole new way, as well as how to use it to get the effects we needed. We pass all these tips along to you within these pages.

We watched each other work and realized how individual this process is—how Nancy's flowers and trees always look different from Natalie's, and how Nancy's color choices are jewel tones and Natalie's are muddy—and how important creative differences are. As we wrote, we wanted to honor that individuality. Therefore, we tried not only to avoid being prescriptive, but also to avoid patterns altogether. The step-by-step directions we give are guidelines only. Within them you can be as innovative as your heart desires. We give examples of many kinds of landscape quilts to encourage you to take off on your own flight of fancy.

To avoid confusion, we've written descriptions of our various quilts in the third person (Nancy or Natalie), so that you will always know who made which quilt and what she went through to make it. We've also added notes from Nancy or Natalie when we've had individual insights to pass along to you.

What we most want to convey in this book is how much fun it is to make these quilts. We love to make them—and we think we always will. We hope you feel the same after making your first landscape quilt. Have fun!

—Nancy and Natalie

Contents

43

50

76

To my husband, Richard, my most generous critic.
—Natalie

To my sons, Ted and Tom, my valued landscape critics.
—Nancy

105

118

131

1

Getting Started

Remember when you were a child how you loved to cut out pretty pictures and paste them onto colored paper to create a scene? That's what you'll do when you make your landscape quilt—except, of course, you'll cut your pretty pictures from fabric and attach them to a fabric background.

A landscape quilt is fabric art in which the quilter/artist reproduces the beauty of nature. The quilt may feature a flower or a rock garden, a forest, a meadow, a lake or a river, the seashore, a snowy mountain peak, or any other landscape scene.

When you look at the quilt at left, with its intricate blossoms and leaves, you may think you're gazing at a painting—and you might get the idea that this technique is too difficult for you. Nothing could be further from the truth!

Alaine's Window **by Natalie Sewell (42" x 54")**

Looking for Inspiration

Before you begin your landscape quilt, you will first need to find a photo or a picture for inspiration. Look for a scene you would like to see out your window—or better still, one you would like to have hanging on your wall.

Find the Focal Point

The focus of your quilt should be interesting and easy to re-create. Avoid such objects as intricate statues or ornate grillwork; they are difficult to reproduce in fabric. A simple birdbath or wooden fence is a good choice. If a photo you like contains a complicated element, substitute a simpler one from another picture.

Be Flexible

The photo is simply a starting place for your landscape quilt, so feel free to eliminate or add anything you choose. Ignore that row of delphiniums or that reflecting pool, for example. Depending on what you like and which kind of fabrics you have in your stash, you can change the scene any way you choose. Remember, you're simply looking for inspiration.

Note from Natalie: Even though I'm a gardener with flower beds constantly on the brain, I still need a concrete illustration with shadow and shape to get me started on a new landscape quilt. A good photo shows me the relative sizes of various flowers and the intricate shade spots that my memory can't recall.

Study the Light

Note the position of the sun in your photo, what time of day it is, and how deep the shadows are. Given the fabrics you have, can you reproduce these effects?

From Photo to Fabric

Inspirational scenes are everywhere, from greeting cards to magazine photography to your own backyard. Here are some of the photos that inspired Natalie's quilts.

Black-eyed Susans
(49" x 35")

The photo at right (by Beth and John Ross of Madison, Wisconsin) has the elegant simplicity and dark mood Natalie was looking for to inspire a quilt made with yellow daisy fabric from her stash. The photo has three elements: flowers, grass, and a dark background. Natalie combined daisy fabric with some grass print for the garden and used a dark gray/blue hand-dyed fabric for the background.

Compare the photo and the quilt, and you'll see that Natalie didn't follow the photo exactly. One thing that attracted her to the photo was the contrast of the background with the grasses; therefore, Natalie's quilt features much more sky than you see in the photo. (See pages 30–35 for step-by-step instructions.)

Alaine's Window
(42" x 54")

The photo (far left) was the inspiration for Natalie's first flower garden quilt. She calls it *Alaine's Window* in honor of the photographer, Alaine Johnson, of Stoughton, Wisconsin. In truth, Alaine simply propped an old window up in her sister's garden and shot the photo; but the effect is one of a window opening into an English garden.

Natalie's fabric stash contained none of the flowers in the photo, but she learned that substitutions can be just as charming. In making this quilt, she also learned how many more leaves than flowers are needed to make a landscape quilt. Another lesson learned in making her first landscape quilt: A dark background enhances the bright colors of the flowers.

The Birdbath
(53" x 41")

Natalie took this photo in her own backyard during a time of year when little was in bloom. She remedied the bloom problem with an abundance of florals from her fabric stash. Natalie also felt that the birdbath in the photo was too ornate to reproduce, so she drew inspiration from a simpler replacement found in a garden catalog. A piece of hand-dyed fabric became the water in the birdbath; notice how the "water" seems to reflect the sky. The dark spots in the photo inspired Natalie to leave dark spots in the background of her quilt, too.

Trillium
(42" x 34")

This photo, taken by Nancy, inspired Natalie's quilt that features the delicate blooms of the trillium. Instead of reproducing the green background of Nancy's photo, Natalie used a hand-dyed mauve piece that she had just purchased. "The fabric suggested to me the color of the earth before spring emerges," says Natalie. "Nancy's photo was invaluable for making the blossoms and leaves and for suggesting the nature of a clump of trillium. But I departed from the photo when I invented the log, the brown leaves, and the background." (See pages 72 and 73 for step-by-step instructions for making *Trillium*.)

Fabric Selection

Choosing fabrics for a quilt is very much like choosing the right hues for a painting. Although there are few wrong choices, the following tips may help you choose more effectively.

Background Fabrics

One of the first things you need to learn before making a landscape quilt is that the sky isn't always blue. Leaf through garden books or seed catalogs, and you'll see that most of the photos have dark backgrounds. Often, the background is comprised of shadows formed from adjacent shrubbery. This gives the flowers a special glow. As we saw in the photos that inspired *Black-eyed Susans, Alaine's Window,* and *The Birdbath* (pages 10 and 11), the dark background illuminates the foliage.

Nancy and Natalie's preference for background fabrics is mottled, dark textures. Solids are taboo, as they are too static and stop any movement in your scene.

Hand-dyed fabrics are a great choice because of the irregularity of texture; also the high contrast of light and dark streaks and smudges can look like mulch and shrubs and foliage in the shade. Because each piece is unique, hand-dyed fabrics add to the one-of-a-kind nature of your work. Hand-dyes are becoming more readily available to quilters throughout the country; if none are available in your area, you may be able to purchase them through catalogs and Internet sources. Although they can be more expensive than commercial fabrics, hand-dyes are well worth the extra cost. (See "Resources" on page 143 for sources of hand-dyed fabrics.)

Enhance the bright colors of floral prints with dark background fabrics.

Fabric Artist: Sharon Luehring, Confetti Works

Since hand-dyed fabrics have contributed so much to the appearance of the landscape quilts featured in this book, credit goes to those artists whose fabrics have been used the most.

Sharon Luehring, creator of Confetti Works hand-dyed fabrics, uses 100%-cotton broadcloth dyed with Procion® fiber reactive dyes. (See "Resources" on page 143.)

Floral Fabrics

Choose floral fabrics by looking at the flowers themselves and not at the leaves or the background color. The leaves are rarely adequate in floral fabrics. Most often, you'll be substituting leaves from other fabrics that feature only leaves. After you cut out the flowers, the leaves and the background will frequently become only scraps on the sewing room floor.

Note from Natalie: In the same amount of space, fabrics tend to feature 30 flowers for every three in nature. If you put too many flowers in your quilt design, you will make something that looks like wallpaper or—even less desirable—like more floral fabric. Nature is much more sparse with her flowers.

Try to find floral fabrics that show flowers at a variety of angles. Look for flower shapes that can be made into clumps—letting some obscure parts of others, hiding some behind leaves, and facing others sideways or backwards. If you can't find buds in the fabric, look for mature flowers that you can cut into buds.

Watch your scale. Four-inch roses won't work with one-inch zinnias. The flowers you pick from various fabrics need to look as if they could grow next to each other. It's fairly easy to reduce the size of some flowers by cutting off the outer layer of petals. If they're too small to begin with, they're useless.

Mix a wide variety of colors and textures of floral fabrics. Many of the best florals have more than one kind of flower that will work. When planning a new quilt, gather a wide variety of floral fabrics—some impressionistic, some realistic, some more abstract—and group the flowers together in the scene. Also try to use a wide variety of colors—red next to pink and purple, some orange, a spot of yellow or white, and a few splashes of violet blue.

Note from Natalie: Let me warn you: Landscape quilting may require a lot of fabric shopping and a large fabric stash! If I can't find the shade I need in fabric, I enhance the color with fabric markers or fabric paint. The shading in an original flower will come through the fabric paint, and the effect is wonderful.

Go for a variety of textures and scales when selecting your floral fabrics.

Foliage Fabric

Leaves and shrubs will take up the most space in your quilt, so selecting the right foliage fabric for your garden quilt is very important. For distant foliage, mottled batiks in many hues are good. But for close-up leaves, distinct leaf shapes that you can cut out are necessary. Make sure the scale of the leaves suits the flowers they will accompany. Try not to worry too much about botanical accuracy, but do stay consistent within each quilt. That is, if you pick a certain leaf to accompany a peony blossom, stay with that kind of leaf each time you add a peony.

Every leaf fabric should have at least five different shades of coloration, ranging from light to dark. That way, you'll guarantee some dappled light in your scene, creating the illusion that the sun is playing on parts of the leaves while leaving other parts in the shade. Avoid calicos with only two or three hues. From a distance they will appear flat and look unnatural. Use both right and wrong sides of a leaf fabric to create a sense of sunshine and shadow, and you'll get two fabrics for the price of one.

You can never have enough shades of green in your quilt. If you look at a lot of gardens and garden photos, you'll notice that yellow-greens, teals, and olives all go together. Nature is filled with marvelous variations of green, and those variations give your scene depth and dimension.

Rock Fabrics

Although you'll probably use rock fabric sparingly, rocks in garden beds add important texture to the scene. Look for prints with various shades of gray and brown. Tweed-looking prints often make excellent rocks. Cut rock fabrics jagged and rough; turn the fabric over frequently to suggest the interplay of sunshine and shadow.

Use a variety of colors and shapes for your foliage.

Remember that gray prints make excellent rocks.

Tools and Notions

As with any sewing or quilting project, landscape quilting requires specific tools and notions. The list is short, but important. See Nancy's Notions on page 144 to order any of the products shown.

Scissors

Scissors—4" to 5" in length—with extremely sharp points are critical for landscape quilting. Because cutting fabric will be one of the main steps, sharp-pointed scissors that are comfortable to your hand are essential *(Photo A)*.

Rotary Cutter, Mat, and Ruler

You'll use this cutting trio primarily when squaring the quilt top and cutting borders and backing fabrics *(Photo B)*. Make certain that the cutter has a sharp blade.

Sewing/Craft Glue Stick

Gluing is a key step in creating a landscape quilt *(Photo C)*. You'll need several sticks of glue for each quilt top. Test the glue by applying a consistent layer on a scrap of fabric; if the glue does not easily glide on the fabric, try another brand.

Fabric Adhesive Spray

Another gluing option is to spray the backs of cutouts with a fabric adhesive spray *(Photo D)*. There are many brand names, but all fabric sprays work the same.

Pellon Fleece™

The batting we recommend is 100%-polyester fleece by Pellon™. It has the proper loft to provide dimension without bulk and lies flat against the wall.

Safety Pins

Choose size #1 safety pins for securing the quilt layers. There are two options in safety pins: the traditional straight pins or curved pins, shown in *Photo E*, that are designed for easier insertion into the fabric.

A

B

C

D

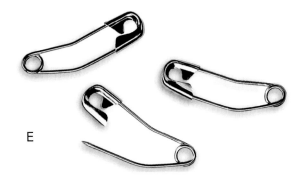

E

Fabric Paints

Paints add depth and character to landscape designs. Choose acid-free, nontoxic, permanent markers *(Photo F)*. Use the markers to highlight and to shade various areas of the fabric, to darken leaves or petals, or to change the color of a chosen feature.

Thread and Needles

Use a transparent nylon thread for free-motion quilting *(Photo G)*. The clear thread blends in with the fabric, eliminating the need to change thread colors when stitching on various fabrics. Use the nylon thread as the top thread and an all-purpose thread that matches the background fabric in the bobbin.

Experiment with needle selection. Generally, a size 80 (12) Universal point needle is used for quilting. If the thread breaks, switch to a metallic or Metalfil needle, which has a longer eye that prevents the thread from breaking or shredding.

F

G

Darning Foot or Big Foot®

Many machines include a darning foot in their accessory boxes. Such a foot is generally clear, allowing you to see where you're going and also where you've been *(Photo H)*. The foot is designed with a shorter shank height, which allows you to move the fabric freely under the foot area while providing sufficient surface contact with the fabric.

Available separately is Big Foot, a giant darning foot with a larger foot area, which provides a greater area of surface contact *(Photo I)*.

H

I

Quilt Sew Easy™

Landscape quilts are stitched in two phases: 1) free-motion machine stitching the elements to the background fabric, and 2) free-motion quilting the top, batting, and backing layers. Natalie and Nancy recommend Quilt Sew Easy when free-motion stitching. This flexible hoop sits on the top of the quilt; its foam underside allows you to hold the fabric with tight control, as if you were holding a steering wheel *(Photo J)*. You can reposition it by simply lifting the hoop to another area of the quilt.

J

Rubber Fingers

Used by office staff and available at office supply stores, rubber fingers allow you to move the fabric with ease while free-motion stitching. Wear the rubber tips on your index and middle fingers *(Photo K)*.

Quilting Tables

When quilting your landscape project, you'll need an extended flat working surface. If your machine does not have a work surface larger than the machine itself, consider investing in a portable table that fits around the free arm of your machine *(Photo L)* or in a cabinet that has a large extended surface.

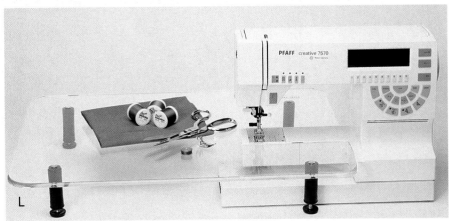

Bias Bars

When designing landscape quilts with the look of stained glass, use bias trim accents for lattice or vines. Follow instructions with bias bars to create custom-made bias trim with your choice of fabric *(Photo M)*. The metal or plastic bars make the bias trim uniform in width.

Quick Bias

Another option for a stained-glass effect is to use ready-made bias trim, such as Quick Bias *(Photo N)*. This ¼" trim has a fusible web on the underside, making it easy to temporarily position the trim on the landscape background.

Sewing Machine

If you spend a considerable amount of time at your sewing machine, you'll want a high-quality machine that makes piecing and quilting a breeze. Nancy uses a Pfaff 7570 *(Photo O),* which has an exclusive dual feed. You will need to make a few adjustments to your machine for landscape quilting, as indicated in the photo below.

Reduce upper tension by two numbers.

Thread needle with clear monofilament thread.

Adjust machine for straight stitching.

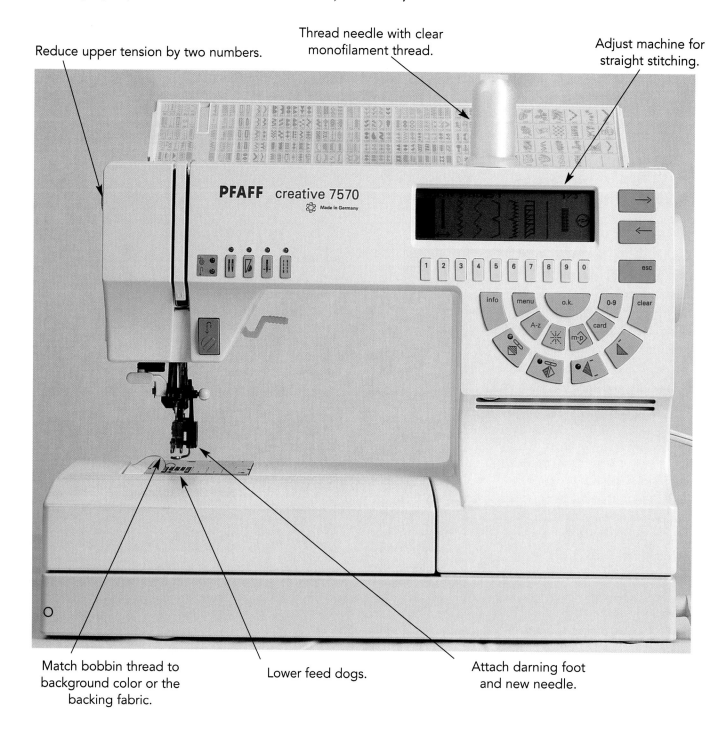

Match bobbin thread to background color or the backing fabric.

Lower feed dogs.

Attach darning foot and new needle.

Basic Techniques

*After you've chosen a photo and the fabric for your quilt,
there are four basic techniques you need to know to make the quilts
in this book: cutting and gluing, machine-stitching the quilt top,
squaring up the quilt top, and adding borders.*

Note from Nancy: Experienced quilters and sewers may think they can skim over these basic steps. Take it from one who had those very thoughts: it's truly important to follow these steps as outlined by Natalie. I smugly thought that I didn't really need to glue each design element as diligently as Natalie taught me. Guess what? I now glue following these guidelines, and my results have greatly improved.

The icons below represent the basic techniques used in this book. When you see one of these and the accompanying page number, refer to that page for instructions on the technique.

"Cutting and Gluing" on page 20.

"Machine-Stitching the Quilt Top" on page 21.

"Squaring Up the Quilt Top" on page 23.

"Adding Borders" on page 24.

Studying the basics now will help you plan your landscape quilt successfully, from cutting and gluing to adding the finishing touches.

Cutting and Gluing

Cutting and gluing are the first steps to landscape quilting. Follow the instructions below to cut your motifs and to attach them temporarily to your background fabric.

Messy Cutting

When you messy-cut, forget everything you've ever learned about cutting. Cut as poorly as possible, cutting in and out to make jagged edges *(Photo A)*. The secret is to cut badly—hence the name, messy cutting. Messy cutting is used primarily for distant woodland scenes involving both foliage and ground cover (chapters 5 and 6). It is also used to create distant foliage in some sections of close-up flower garden quilts (chapters 2, 3, and 4).

Fussy Cutting

Fussy cutting is used for leaves and flowers that are relatively close-up. You'll be following the lines of the printed motifs in the fabric and carefully cutting them out. Trim portions of the fabric between flowers that are not part of the blooms *(Photo B)*. This will take some time, but it is important for the look of your quilt.

Note from Natalie: Fussy cutting can be tedious work. I can't stand at the design wall (see page 26) and cut endless leaves and blossoms, so I save this task for evening TV or long car rides. It's much more fun to design at the wall with dozens of precut leaves, blossoms, and grasses in hand.

Gluing

Place a fabric motif you've cut out right side down on a large scrap of leftover batting. The batting keeps the fabric motif from shifting and protects your worktable from glue. Apply a consistent layer of glue from a sewing/craft glue stick over the entire back of the motif, extending over the fabric edges *(Photo C)*.

Another way to attach fabric motifs to the background fabric is to use a fabric adhesive spray. Simply place several fabric pieces right side down on the batting and lightly spray the backs of the motifs. Since the spray has a wider coverage, it is best to coat several pieces at the same time.

Note from Nancy: Glue sticks are traditionally used for paper, so a little dab won't do! We've noticed that many beginning landscape quilters tend to scrimp on the amount of glue they use and feel very frustrated when the pieces they positioned so carefully fly off when they move the quilt top to the sewing machine. You need to apply glue over the entire outer edges of each motif so that the motif will stay in place when it's positioned on the background.

Note from Natalie: There are many fabric stabilizers on the market that iron onto one fabric and adhere easily to another fabric. Don't use these on your landscape quilts. They stiffen the fabrics they're used on and decrease the loft of trees and flowers when they are machine quilted.

Machine-Stitching the Quilt Top

Glue temporarily holds the various quilt elements together, allowing you to rearrange them. Once you're satisfied with the design, machine-stitch the pieces to the background fabric to keep all the sections permanently in place.

Set up your sewing machine for free-motion embroidery or stitching.

- Lower your feed dogs. (Check your owner's manual if you are unsure of how to make this adjustment.)
- Reduce the upper tension by two numbers or notches.
- Insert a Universal or Metafil needle (see page 16). Test your needle on your fabric to make sure it is making the smallest hole possible; adjust your needle size accordingly. Some fabrics are denser and do better with a smaller needle.
- Thread the needle with a nylon monofilament thread.
- Match the bobbin thread to the background color. If you can't decide among several colors, choose the one that's slightly darker than your background fabric. It will show less.
- Adjust the machine for a straight stitch.
- Attach a darning foot, shown below, or a specialty foot such as the Big Foot®, shown on page 16.

Darning
Foot

Machine-baste around the shapes to hold the outer edges in place.

- Use rubber fingers (shown in the photo below), available from office supply stores, to control the fabric. An alternative method is to insert the fabric in a hoop; however, this method requires removing and reattaching the hoop several times to cover the entire quilt top. Or use a Quilt Sew Easy™ hoop. Place the hoop, sponge side down, for easy gripping. The hoop is easy to reposition as you baste the quilt top. (See page 16 for more information.)
- Lower the presser foot to the darning or sewing position. The foot will glide slightly above the fabric.

- Place your hands evenly on both sides of the needle, gently holding the quilt top in place, as shown below.
- Guide the fabric with your hands. Since the feed dogs are lowered, you—and not your machine—will be controlling the fabric.
- Move the fabric at an even speed under the presser foot area.

Note from Nancy: If you've never used free-motion stitching, we suggest you practice on scrap material before working on your quilt.

Use rubber fingers to control the fabric.

- Stitch along the cut edges just enough to anchor the pieces firmly in place.

If you stay close to the edges, you will not have to remove this basting later on *(Diagram A)*.

Steam the quilt top.
- After basting the motifs in place, steam-iron the entire quilt top, pressing on the wrong side to prevent melting the monofilament thread *(Diagram B)*.
- If puckers appear, flatten them with the steam iron. Or break the threads with your seam ripper and flatten the area with more steam *(Diagram C)*.

Note from Natalie: Be a fuss-budget about puckers at this point in the quiltmaking process. You won't have another chance to get rid of them.

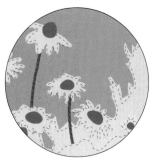

Diagram A

Diagram B

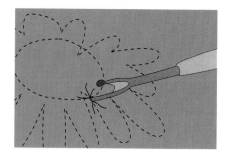

Diagram C

Machine-baste the pieces to the background fabric to keep all the sections in place.

Squaring Up the Quilt Top

It's important to make sure your quilt top is a perfect rectangle before you add borders. Follow the instructions below for perfectly square corners.

Squaring

Squaring your quilt's edges is a vitally important step. Unless it has accurate 90° corners, your quilt will not lie flat. And if it doesn't lie flat, it will not look good hanging on your wall. Take all the time you need to do this step properly.

Diagram A

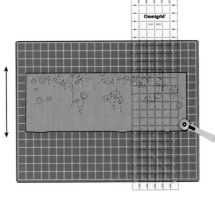

Diagram B

- Fold the quilt top in half, meeting the top and bottom edges *(Diagram A)*.
- Place the quilt top on a cutting mat and align the fold with one of the marked lines on the mat. Using a ruler and a rotary cutter, trim the left and right edges (top and bottom of quilt), making certain you are cutting parallel to the fold *(Diagram B)*.
- Unfold the quilt top and refold it in the opposite direction, meeting side edges. Trim side edges, again cutting parallel to the fold using a rotary cutter and ruler *(Diagram C)*.
- Unfold the quilt top and use a large square ruler to check that each corner is square—that is, each corner should be a 90° angle. If necessary, repeat the folding and trimming process until all corners measure perfect 90° angles *(Diagram D)*.
- Pin the quilt top to your design wall (see page 26). Check and recheck the squareness of the quilt by measuring from the top to the bottom, from left to right, and from corner to corner.
- Steam the quilt with your iron, pressing from the wrong side to flatten and stabilize the quilt top *(Diagram E)*. Let the quilt dry.

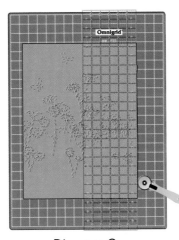

Diagram C

Diagram D

Diagram E

Adding Borders

A landscape quilt's border serves the same purpose as the frame of a picture—it directs attention to the scene. Follow the instructions below to accurately cut, stitch, and miter borders for your quilt.

Auditioning borders and selecting colors will be explained within the following chapters. The basics of stitching the borders and mitering the corners, two important steps that enhance the quilt's appearance, are explained here.

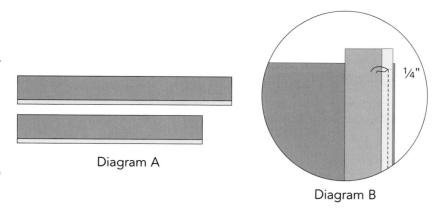

Diagram A

Diagram B

Cutting the Borders

- Cut two outer border lengths and two inner border lengths a minimum of 8" longer than the top and bottom measurement of the quilt.
- Cut two outer border lengths and two inner border lengths a minimum of 8" longer than the side measurement of the quilt.
- Cut outer borders ½" wider than the desired finished width of the border. Cut inner borders 1" wide.
- Stitch the inner borders to the outer borders with a ¼" seam, as shown in *Diagram A*. Press the seams toward the outer borders.

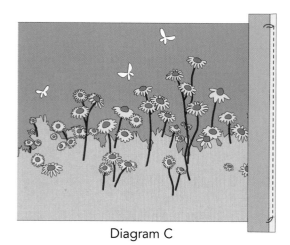

Diagram C

Mitering the Borders

- Pin the borders to the sides of the quilt top, with right sides together.
- Place a mark on the side borders, ¼" from each corner of the quilt top and bottom. Stitch from mark to mark, using a ¼" seam allowance *(Diagrams B and C)*.
- Repeat, pinning and stitching the borders to the top and the bottom of the quilt, again stopping the stitching ¼" from each corner and allowing 3" to 4" extensions at each end.
- Form the miters, working with one corner at a time. Press the borders right side out to the finished position *(Diagram D)*.

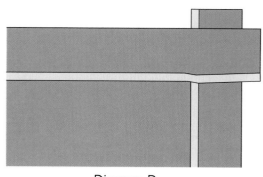

Diagram D

- Smooth one of the corner borders flat. Fold the adjoining border, aligning the outer edges of the two border strips to create a 45° mitered corner. Press along the fold *(Diagram E)*.

- Pin the borders together at the mitered edge. Fold back the quilt top, exposing the wrong side and the press mark *(Diagram F)*.

- Stitch along the press mark, sewing to the point of the miter. Trim seam allowances to ¼" *(Diagram G)*. Press open the seam *(Diagram H)*.

- Repeat to miter each corner.

- After borders are added, you can glue and stitch more motifs, letting them overlap onto the borders for added effect (see the photo below).

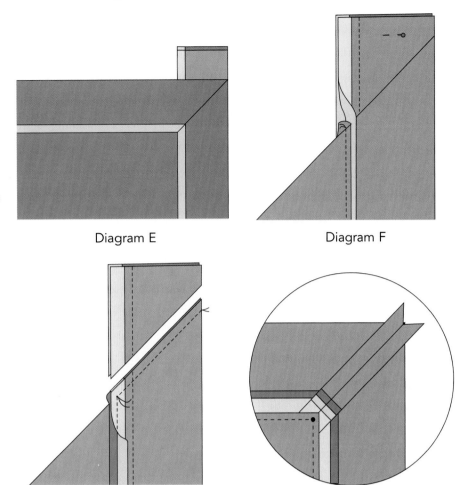

Diagram E

Diagram F

Natalie added some of the flowers, the grasses, and the butterflies after stitching the borders in place, letting these motifs overlap the borders for added interest.

Diagram G

Diagram H

Design Wall Options

*Since landscape quilts are made to hang on a wall, it's important
to design your landscape quilt while working on a vertical surface. You will be able
to step back, view your design, and determine if the scene is to your liking.
Working on a vertical surface also encourages suggestions from family and friends.*

Making a Permanent Design Wall

If your home allows for it, having a permanent design wall in your sewing area can be a marvelous tool for landscape quilting. Make yours as big as the space allows.

Supplies

- Corkboard, 65" x 112" or as big as space will permit
- Café curtain drapery rod (112" or as long as your wall space permits horizontally)
- Twin-size bed batting (thick)
- Three or four brackets to support drapery rod
- Twin-size flannel flat sheet (preferably white or cream)

Assembly

1. Nail or screw a corkboard to your wall at easel height. Along the top wall of the cork surface, tack a thick twin-size bed batting.

2. At the top corners of the board, install a drapery rod. Support the drapery rod in the middle as well as at both ends with brackets *(Diagram A)*.

3. Create a sleeve pocket along one side of a white or cream-colored flannel twin–sized flat sheet and hang it on the café curtain rod. (If necessary, shorten the sheet to fit the cork board surface.) The flannel covering makes an ideal surface for fabric pieces—and the combination of the flannel and the thick batting allows for easy pinning of quilts and quilt tops *(Diagram B)*.

Natalie's design wall at home covers two windows.

Note from Natalie: My design wall covers two windows. Instead of using cork board, I chose pine board, a much heavier piece of wood to accommodate the fluctuations in my wall. If you will be placing this board on a standard drywall surface, corkboard is easier to work with; if not, you now know a substitution.

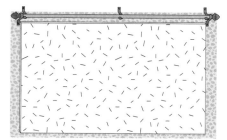

Diagram A

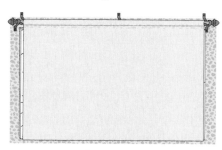

Diagram B

Making a Portable Design Wall

If you're a beginning fabric landscape artist or have no space for a permanent design wall, consider making a portable design wall. It can double as a pressing surface. Donna Fenske—a sewing and quilting designer who works at Nancy's Notions—designed this simple project. Construction takes about 30 minutes.

Supplies

- 1 yard of Iron Quick Teflon-Coated Fabric
- 1⅛ yards of cotton flannel
- 48" or longer curtain rod or wooden dowel

Assembly

1. Square the edges of the Iron-Quick to a true rectangle with a rotary cutter, rulers, and board to assure that the fabric edges are straight (see page 23).

2. Cut the flannel the same width as the Iron-Quick plus 4" longer to provide a rod pocket.

3. Meet the Iron-Quick and the flannel, right sides together, with the flannel extending 4" at the top. Stitch a ¼" seam along the sides and the lower edge *(Diagram C)*.

4. Turn the fabric right sides out. Turn under ¼" on the unstitched edge of the flannel.

5. Fold the flannel down over the Iron-Quick and stitch the folded edge in place to form a rod pocket *(Diagram D)*.

6. Insert a dowel or a rod into the rod pocket. Hang the design surface with the flannel side out. The Teflon backing allows you to also press on this surface.

A portable design wall is an excellent design tool. You can use it to take a work-in-progress to a friend's house to get her opinion or to a quilt shop to select fabrics.

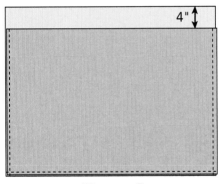

Diagram C

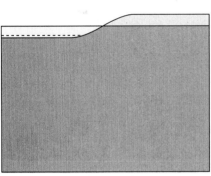

Diagram D

2

Creating Your Own Landscape Quilt

To show you how to create a landscape quilt, we'll re-create Natalie's *Black-eyed Susans* shown at left. You can apply these techniques to make any landscape quilt you desire. You'll master techniques for selecting appropriate fabrics, cutting the shapes you need, layering pieces, and adding dimensional elements—such as butterflies that seem to float off the quilt.

As you're working on your quilt, it's important to step back periodically and view your design from a distance to get the right perspective. That's really only possible if you work on a vertical design wall. For help with creating a design wall, see pages 26 and 27.

Black-eyed Susans **by Natalie Sewell**
(49" x 35")

Creating *Black-eyed Susans*

In this chapter, we describe in detail how
Natalie created her Black-eyed Susans *quilt. Use the same*
steps to design and make your own landscape quilt.

The Inspiration

The photo shown at right inspired *Black-eyed Susans*. Notice
that there are only three main elements in the photo—the
background, the flowers, and the grasses. Natalie re-created the
scene using relatively few fabrics. Remember that the photo is
only a starting point; you will never be able to duplicate it, nor
would you want to. But having it on hand will make your creative process a lot easier, especially in the beginning.

Photo by Beth and John Ross of Madison, Wisconsin

Background Fabric

Choose a background fabric that is mottled and variegated (see the photo below). Avoid solids and remember that the sky does not have to be blue. For our background fabric, we chose a yard of Sharon Luehring's hand-dyed gray (see "Resources" on page 143). It's mottled with dark and light splotches and conveys a sense of both sky and distant foliage.

Foliage Fabric

Next, select two foliage prints: one to represent grasses and the second—preferably a variegated hand-dyed print in shades of green—for larger grasses. Of the foliage prints below, the one on the left features several kinds of grasses. Even though the grass types are quite different from that in the photo, the mood and the effect are similar. The mottled brown-and-black print in the center forms the dark areas at the bottom left and right of the quilt. The foliage print on the right is a piece of hand-dyed green, which we then cut into slivers. Because of its gradations of color, it looks as if the sun is hitting it in various spots.

Floral Fabric

Next, look for a floral print that approximates black-eyed Susans. Remember, you can use fabric paint to change or intensify the appearance of the flowers. The floral fabrics we chose for the black-eyed Susans have many brilliantly colored flowers; some of them are actually black-eyed Susans. Some are smaller yellow daisies; with sharp scissors and some brown fabric paint, however, they easily became smaller black-eyed Susans in the distance.

Background Fabric

Floral Fabrics

Foliage Fabrics

Creating Your Background Canvas

Your next step is to cut your background fabric to the desired size. *Black-eyed Susans* is 49" across by 35" down. Feel free to work with any size you like, but remember that smaller is not necessarily easier. You will need to scale your quilt to the size of the flowers and the foliage in the fabrics you've chosen to work with. Use a rotary cutter and a ruler to cut your background fabric; then press the fabric and pin it to your design wall at the height best suited to you. Now you're ready to cut and glue your scene.

 Read "Cutting and Gluing Techniques" on page 20 before continuing.

Creating Foliage for *Black-eyed Susans*

- Measure a piece of the grass fabric big enough to cover approximately one half of your background fabric.
- Messy-cut the top edge of the grass fabric, following some of the grasses depicted in the fabric. Move your scissors up and down to create a very rough terrain.
- Glue your grass fabric to your background fabric *(Photo A)*. Remember to apply the glue stick (or adhesive spray) very generously, especially on the messy-cut top edge, as well as on the sides and the bottom of the grass fabric.
- Messy-cut extra grasses from your variegated green fabric. Make slivers with your sharp scissors, taking care to cut from a variety of shades of green to create a sun-drenched look. Glue the slivers on the wrong side and place them randomly on the grass fabric *(Photos B1, B2, and B3)*.
- Messy-cut random scraps of foliage fabric, remembering to cut unevenly. Avoid cloud and lollipop shapes; they won't look natural. Glue and position them on the grass fabric.

Messy-cut random scraps of foliage fabric.

Creating Flowers for *Black-eyed Susans*

Now that you have your background in place, it's time to add the black-eyed Susans to the piece. Take a good long look at your floral fabric—if it's like most florals, it's quite busy. Single out one flower at a time and mentally note the importance of finding a variety of angles and sizes in the flower type you have chosen. This is a good time to study the variety of flower shapes, angles, and sizes in your inspirational photograph.

Glue and position your flowers onto the foliage and the background.

- Use fabric paint or fabric markers to enhance the chosen flowers before you cut them out. Darken and raise the center disks of the flowers—so that they protrude—by cutting off the top segment of petals *(Photo C)*. Intensify the rays or the petals with yellow or gold paint or markers.
- Cut out the flowers carefully; feel free to reduce the number of petals of some to make each flower a little different from the others. Remember to vary the angles and the sizes of the flowers you have chosen.
- Glue and position your flowers onto the foliage and the background. Some taller ones may extend above the foliage onto the background. Clump the flowers irregularly, leaving a few bare spots here and there. Tuck a few behind some grasses or other blossoms *(Photos D1 and D2)*. Remember that you can pull off temporarily glued pieces as necessary and then reglue them until you are happy with your design.
- Add stems to your flowers. Some flowers won't need stems, as the grasses appear to cover the areas where the stems would appear. For flowers that do need stems, use the same variegated green fabric you used for individual grasses above *(Photo E1 and E2)*. These stems will be skinny; cut them on the bias to enhance the sense that they are twisting in the wind; then glue them very carefully, as they tend to tear under the pressure of the glue stick.

Add stems to your flowers.

Creating Dimensional Butterflies

- Iron the fusible web to the wrong side of the butterfly fabric, using a medium temperature iron.
- Referring to *Photo F,* roughly cut out a butterfly, leaving a ½" margin of fabric.
- Cut an identical fused butterfly.
- Peel off the paper backing of the fusible web. With the wrong sides together, fuse the two layers of the two butterflies together with a medium temperature iron.
- Trim the excess from the back of the fused butterfly.
- Stitch the center of the butterfly body to the quilt after quilting *(Photo G).*

Note from Natalie: I added some simple cabbage butterflies to my quilt. Using a plastic template, I drew them on a piece of mottled white fabric and then positioned them on the background fabric. They are flat rather than three-dimensional.

Choosing Other Flowers

Feel free to use any flower you like to create your scene. Perhaps you don't have any daisy-shaped flowers that can double as black-eyed Susans. Or maybe you prefer sunflowers, roses, zinnias, or dahlias. Just remember the basic principles: Watch your scale and choose flowers that have a variety of angles and sizes and that can be clumped in a natural way. Also look for appropriate foliage. Roses, for example, need branching bushes, not grasses. But as long as you are consistent, you need not adhere to strict botanical accuracy.

See *"Machine-Stitching the Quilt Top"* on page 21 for more information.

See *"Squaring Up the Quilt Top"* on page 23 for more information.

See *"Adding Borders"* on page 24 for more information.

Auditioning Borders for *Black-eyed Susans*

Landscape quilts can be very busy scenes and, like oil paintings and watercolors, need the peace and quiet of calm borders. A border fabric should give a sense of serenity to the piece *(Photo H)*. Cutting your border from your background fabric can be effective. But if you do this, you will need a ½" to 1"-wide finished inner border of a contrasting color to set it off *(Photo I)*.

Border width can vary, of course, depending on the size of the quilt. A 4"-wide border is very pleasing on a 65" x 52" quilt, but the same size border would overwhelm a smaller quilt.

The only way to choose the color and the size of a border is to audition one. Pin your quilt top on the vertical design wall and try out a variety of fabrics in various widths to find the one that works best. Leave the borders you are auditioning up next to your quilt top for a while. What seems to work well in the evening may not look so good the next morning. Note that after the borders were sewn on, we added flowers, grasses, and butterflies, letting them overlap the borders. This gives the quilt even more dimension.

Note from Nancy: For me, choosing borders is the most difficult part of the landscape quilting process. I have been known to finish a landscape quilt, realize the border was wrong, and take the quilt apart to add a better border—a process to avoid at all costs. To solve my dilemmas, I ask my good friend Natalie for help in choosing the right border fabric. I recommend you consult a friend or a family member for opinions. This person does not have to have knowledge of quilting, just an appreciation of color.

Another option is to eliminate the border completely. This gives the quilt a very contemporary look. After layering and machine-quilting the piece, finish it by binding it with the same fabric used for the background or one slightly darker (see page 136 for binding instructions).

The Rock Garden by Natalie Sewell
(41" x 33")

Creating
The Rock Garden

The inspiration for *The Rock Garden* came from a photo accompanying a garden column in the local newspaper one spring. The hand-dyed background fabric in the quilt is impressionistic—the foreground and the distance are left up to the viewer's imagination. Turn the page to see the step-by-step process by which this quilt was constructed.

Choosing Fabric

Natalie created *The Rock Garden* using only a few fabrics. Choose a dark, mottled hand-dyed fabric for your background. It will give the impression of distant foliage and close-up mulch. Select three or four foliage fabrics with small-scale leaves, three or four small-scale floral prints, a larger tulip print, and a green batik for tulip leaves. Pick a tweedy print for the rocks or cut out rock shapes from a gray fabric, like the background of the muted tulip print. Often, the wrong side of a floral print will work for a rock. Watch your scale when selecting these fabrics. Remember that you will need many more leaves than flowers to make this scene look realistic.

Background Fabric

Background Foliage Fabrics

Floral Fabrics

Creating the Background
- Cut your background fabric to the desired size of your quilt.
- Pin your background fabric to the vertical design wall.

 See "Cutting and Gluing Techniques" on page 20 before continuing.

Creating Distant Foliage
- Messy-cut background foliage. You will be starting to work on your design at the upper left-hand corner of the quilt so choose small-scale prints of foliage. Remember, this is the background of the design; it would appear farther away if you were actually viewing it in nature.
- Cut shapes to denote foliage areas. Let the fabric designs dictate where you cut. Follow the leaf outlines in the fabric and cut out clusters of leaves. You can do a lot of this cutting while watching TV or traveling and then come to your design wall with dozens of leaves and some ground cover.
- Glue and position the foliage shapes where desired. Working from the upper left to the lower right, create the cascading rock garden. Remember to use a piece of batting under your pieces while you are gluing to protect your worktable and to ensure you are covering all the edges with glue. As you work, tuck the edges of some pieces under those of other pieces. Use darker shades in the distance and as you approach the front, turn the foliage fabric over and use the back (you will be gluing on the right side) to create the sense of sun hitting the leaves *(Photo A)*.

Adding Small Flowers and Additional Background Foliage
- Use small-scale flowers for the background foliage *(Photo B)*. Cut them out with fussy-cutting techniques (see page 20).
- .• Step back and review your design from as far away as possible. Or look at it through a camera lens. If you aren't pleased with part of it, remove that section, reposition it, and reglue it.

Adding Foreground Foliage
- Add foreground foliage and flowers that have been precisely cut out, using fussy-cutting techniques.
- Use larger flowers in the foreground than in the background *(Photo C)*.

- Cut out tulip leaves from a green batik fabric to provide for natural leaf variegation, as well as for the illusion of sunshine and shadows. Remember, in nature, plants and flowers are rarely one solid color. They usually include several variations of green.
- Save time by folding and stacking the fabric and using a rotary cutter and mat (but no ruler) to cut multiple leaves at one time.
- Cut leaves at a bit of an angle rather than perfectly straight. A teardrop shape looks more natural. Cut some leaves on the bias to make it easier to shape them in the design.
- Glue and position the tulip leaves against the background. Use smaller leaves in the distance *(Photo D)*.

Creating the Tulip Shapes

- If the flowers in the fabric are not the color you desire, color them with fabric paint or markers to intensify or change the color before cutting out the blooms *(Photo E)*. If the fabric flower has color variations, those shadings will remain after coloring. Use brighter, more intense colors for those in the foreground, use darker, more subdued colors for tulips that will be in the background, behind other flowers.
- Cut flower shapes following the design in the fabric. Cut flowers precisely to imitate their natural shapes, rather than cutting the less defined shapes used for background areas.
- Reduce the size of flowers that are in the distance to approximately two-thirds that of those in the foreground. To make smaller flowers, cut slightly inside the printed flower outline.
- Create flower buds by using only a fraction of the printed flower shape. Use a small portion of green fabric to make the base of the bud.
- Position the tulips on the background. Creatively turn some of the flowers to make them look natural. Place some flowers straight up; angle others to the right or to the left.
- Add narrow stems after placing flowers on the quilt *(Photo F)*. Some tulips will not need stems since they're hidden behind other leaves.

Adding Rocks and Additional Foreground Foliage

- Fussy-cut rock shapes from a gray tweedy print, such as the one shown on page 14. Rocks tend to have curved, rather than flat, bottoms and tops. Scale is important; make the rocks in proportion to the other parts of the design.
- Tuck some of the rocks under the foliage. Remember that rock gardens tend to cascade down, rather than be strictly horizontal. Add moss-like shapes around the rocks from bits of your foliage fabric.
- Foreground foliage and flowers can be somewhat larger and more distinct than those in the distance. Shapes farther back in the rock garden can be less detailed, with jagged cuts *(Photo G)*.
- Remember, it is not necessary to cover all of the background fabric, which extends into the foreground. The viewer's eye will interpret the background fabric that shows through as mulch, grass, or leaves.

Applying Basic Techniques

- Once you've finished designing your quilt top, you are ready for the next steps: machine-stitching, squaring up the quilt top, and adding the borders.

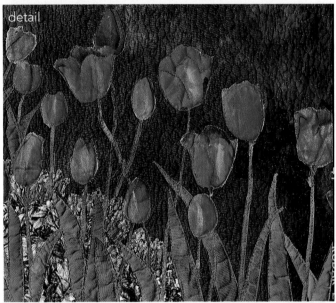

 See *"Machine-Stitching the Quilt Top"* on page 21 for more information.

 See *"Squaring Up the Quilt Top"* on page 23 for more information.

 See *"Adding Borders"* on page 24 for more information.

Auditioning or Eliminating Borders

- At this point in your quiltmaking process, you will need to decide whether to add a border to your rock garden. Natalie left her quilt borderless and simply bound it with the same fabric she used in the background. The quilt takes on a more contemporary look without a border. Also, because the background surrounds the scene, it already has the illusion of a border.
- *Photo H* shows the quilt remade with a border. Notice the ¾" yellow inner border, which highlights the flowers and sets off the outer border made from the same fabric as the background. Because these flower scenes are so busy, a simple matching border, such as this one, seems to add serenity to the scene. Feel free to decide which border works best for your quilt. Note that Natalie stitched on a tulip and a leaf after we added borders, letting them overlap the borders (see page 136 for binding).

Showcase of Flower Garden Quilts

Here are a few more floral landscape quilts that Natalie made using the techniques demonstrated in this chapter.

The *Oriental Floral Panels* suggest a simple alternative to an intricate flower garden. For her background fabric, Natalie chose a yard of hand-dyed fabric by Mickey Lawler, which she calls Sky-dyes (see "Resources" on page 143). Natalie cut the yard in half to make two panels. To make the tropical flower panel (the red and gold flowers of unknown botanical origin at left), she simply cut out the flowers from a floral fabric. She cut the twigs and the branches on the bias from a brown batik (for both panels). The leaves are from a piece of mottled green batik.

The hydrangea blossoms (at right) are cut from a piece of white blossom fabric that has an overall pattern. You can shape these blossoms any way you desire. Using the same fabric Natalie used for the tropical flowers, she cut the leaves somewhat larger to match the blossom size.

Making a simple wall hanging is a lovely way to feature some of your favorite background fabrics and florals without expending a great investment of time or design energy. Hang several together or separately on a wall.

Oriental Floral Panels by Natalie Sewell (18" x 42" each)

Poppies and Butterflies (top, right) was created for Natalie's local botanical garden to help celebrate its first public butterfly hatching. This was also Natalie's first attempt at making meadows and butterflies. For the background, she chose a very dark hand-dyed fabric created by Sharon Luehring, because she wanted her poppies and wildflowers to stand out. Natalie also needed a dark stage on which to let her butterflies—especially the little white ones—shine. She created the grasses for this quilt the same way she did for *Black-eyed Susans* (page 32)—that is, messy-cutting large pieces of grass fabric and gluing them to the background fabric.

The poppies themselves were cut from a variety of flower fabrics. The pink ones came from swatches of upholstery fabric Natalie found on sale at a local store. Because she wanted a wide variety of colors, she changed some of the poppies' hues with fabric paint.

The butterflies were a special challenge. Natalie wanted them to be realistic, since the public was going to witness actual butterflies being hatched. So she bought a butterfly book and copied a few of them onto batik fabric, using fabric markers. The technique for making them three-dimensional is described on page 34.

Natalie created *Tulips on Parade* (bottom, right) one cold, snowy February afternoon while dreaming of spring. The background is a piece of hand-dyed green fabric by Sharon Luehring. It's very mottled and reminded Natalie of new spring grasses. She added sprigs of fabric grasses here and there to create the illusion of a meadow.

The flowers came from three different fabrics. The pale purple tulips were from a new fabric Natalie bought at a local quilt store. She massed 30 purple tulips in the foreground.

The red-and-yellow tulips were cut from a piece of nonfloral batik. With a

***Poppies and Butterflies* by Natalie Sewell (60" x 47")**

***Tulips on Parade* by Natalie Sewell (56" x 41")**

pencil, Natalie drew tulip shapes right on the fabric, starting with bigger tulips in front and decreasing the size as they receded into the background. The irises are from a third fabric; the leaves were cut from a piece of hand-dyed green.

To cut the leaves, Natalie used her

rotary cutter without a ruler. Notice that the background leaves are considerably smaller than those in the foreground. After she added the border, Natalie placed a couple of tulips and an iris so that they spilled over onto the border.

3

Adding Garden Accessories to Your Landscapes

Now that you've learned to create a garden with fabric, let's expand on those techniques by adding some garden accessories. Using Natalie's *White Picket Fence* as inspiration, we'll create a garden fence cascading with flowers. The fence adds a new dimension to landscape quilting by providing a focal point for the flowers.

Careful fabric selection allows you to create a classic white picket fence, a rustic brown fence, or even a wrought-iron fence. As with all landscape quilts, it is often helpful to have an inspirational photo as a starting point.

White Picket Fence by Natalie Sewell
(40" x 44")

Creating *White Picket Fence*

*Many of the same fabric selection tips in Chapter 2 apply to this quilt.
However, because we are using a garden accessory as a focal point,
the following modifications may be helpful.*

Plan the Fence First

Rather than choosing all your fabrics at once, wait to choose
your flower fabrics until after you've built your fence. Other-
wise, the scale may be off, with your flowers and leaves either
too large or too small for the size of your finished fence.

Selecting Fabrics

- For the top background fabric, choose a muted, relatively
  dark fabric that will showcase the design and make the
  flowers stand out (see below). (A light blue sky would
  make the flowers recede and appear pale.) Natalie and
  Nancy prefer either hand-dyed fabrics, commercially pro-
  duced batiks, or other fabrics with mottled hues that create
  the illusion of sunlight breaking through clouds.
- For the lower background fabric that will be behind the
  fence, choose a subtle foliage print that includes lights and
  darks (see below).
- For your fence pickets, choose a white or a wood-tone that
  includes color variations. You will later enhance this effect
  by using black or gray fabric markers.

*See "Cutting and Gluing" on page 20 before
continuing.*

A dark background fabric and
mottled foliage print will make
the flowers show up well.

A white-on-white or
wood-tone fabric
makes a good fence.
You may consider
using the wrong side.

Creating the Background

- Determine the size of your quilt before borders. Natalie's *White Picket Fence* is 36" x 40" without borders. As you construct the quilt, imagine the quilt divided in thirds horizontally. In other words, the sky area will take up the top third of the quilt, and the foliage area will take up the lower two-thirds of the quilt.
- Cut the top dark background fabric the desired width and one-third the desired length of the quilt plus several inches for overlap.
- Cut the bottom foliage background fabric the desired width and two-thirds the desired length of the quilt, again allowing several inches for overlap.
- Messy-cut the top of the lower fabric to look like shrubbery. Apply a line of fabric glue along the top edge of the wrong side of the foliage fabric. Lap the foliage fabric over the lower edge of the top background fabric *(Photo A)*. It's not necessary to sew these layers together now. They will be permanently secured later when the quilt is basted.

Creating the Fence

- Cut a strip of white fabric for the fence's cross board, using a rotary cutter, a ruler, and a mat. The cross board on the sample quilt is 2" wide.
- Apply glue to the cross board and position it *(Photo B)*.

Note from Natalie: I usually don't measure when I'm adding elements to a background fabric; however, when it comes to structural elements like a fence or a window, I measure carefully to get the effect I need.

- Use a rotary cutter and a cutting mat to cut multiple 2" pickets at one time from folded and stacked fabric. Usually strips are cut from the crosswise grain of the fabric. But you may have to cut them from the lengthwise grain for them to look realistic.
- Shape the top of the pickets by meeting lengthwise edges and angle-cutting one end to a point with scissors or with a rotary cutter *(Picket Cutting Diagram)*. All the pickets need not be identical—they definitely aren't in the real world!

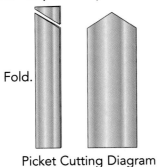

Fold.

Picket Cutting Diagram

- Position and glue the pickets onto the background fabric, spacing them evenly *(Photo C)*. The pickets in *White Picket Fence* are spaced about 1½" apart.
- Referring to *Photo D,* use a fabric marker to add details, highlights, and shadows to the fence. With gray or brown boards, you may want to use black markers, pressing very lightly to create a dark gray tone. With white boards, try using gray.
- Color nail holes in the vertical fence pickets. Create a rust effect around the nail holes by using a brown fabric marker on brown fences and a gray marker on white fences. Test your color choices by trying your nail hole on a fabric scrap.

Choosing Foreground Foliage and Flowers

- Choose four to five flower fabrics and four to five leaf fabrics similar to those shown below. Remember that in nature any color combination goes together. Don't worry about botanical accuracy, but be consistent within the quilt. Use just one kind of leaf for each kind of flower.
- Select fabric prints with the correct scale. If the printed flowers are too large, try reducing the size of the flower by trimming part of the outer edges as you cut.
- Cut out leaves and flowers.

Note from Nancy: Use fussy-cutting techniques for foreground flowers and foliage. Cut precisely, following the leaf and flower outlines. Be sure to trim the fabric between the flowers that is not part of the blooms. This requires a pair of small, sharp-pointed scissors and will take some time.

Fussy-cut leaves from foliage fabrics.

Use several sizes of flowers.

Use small scissors to fussy-cut flowers.

Positioning Flowers and Foliage

- Check garden books, greeting cards, calendars, etc., to aid you in positioning the flowers as they grow naturally *(Photo E)*. Remember to use many more leaves than flowers. You will most likely have to choose leaves from a separate fabric as fabric designers rarely include enough leaves to use in your quilts.

- Apply fabric glue to the backs of the cut out flowers and leaves; then arrange them over and around the fence pickets *(Photo F)*. The background fabric will fill in any remaining areas between the pickets.

- Periodically step back from the quilt top to analyze your design. Add, subtract, or rearrange elements until you are satisfied with the arrangement. Ask for advice from family and friends. You may be surprised at how helpful they can be.

- Once you've finished designing your quilt top, you are ready for the next steps.

 See "Machine-Stitching the Quilt Top" on page 21 for more information.

 See "Squaring the Quilt Top" on page 23 for more information.

 See "Adding Borders" on page 24 for more information.

Showcase of More Picket Fence Quilts

Here are three more picket fence quilts to give you some options and inspiration. Notice the variety of wood in the picket fences and the diversity of flowers and leaves used. You may already have many appropriate fabrics in your collection.

In *The Sunny Side of the Fence,* Natalie chose a gray cedarlike wood for the pickets. This fence scene was designed with elements, such as the background foliage, that give greater dimension and distance. The flowers on this quilt are smaller in scale than those on *White Picket Fence* (see page 46) and climb not only over the fence, but also into the border.

The Sunny Side of the Fence **by Natalie Sewell (32" x 29")**

Natalie took liberties with horticulture to make this quilt. Notice the buds at the top of the quilt on the peony bush—or perhaps it's a rosebush! The fabric did not contain buds, so Natalie cut them from larger flowers. Remember, botanical accuracy is not important. Natalie had fun mixing the vibrant red flowers (species unknown) with the orange petunia-like flowers and the blue hydrangeas.

***Over the Fence* by Natalie Sewell (42" x 54")**

Irises are Nancy's favorite flower, so she made them dominant in this scene. She added ground cover and a few weeds in the front of the fence as well . . . just like at home!

***Irises by the Fence*
by Nancy Zieman
(34" x 30")**

Creating *Sunflowers in the Field*

When Nancy found three different fabrics with three different scales of the same kind of sunflowers, she could not resist the challenge of using them to create depth in a landscape quilt.

***Sunflowers in the Field* by Nancy Zieman (30" x 46")**

Getting Started

Nancy flipped through garden catalogs and found a picture of a field of sunflowers to use as a guide. The snapshot needed a structural element, such as a fence, so she drew in a picket fence. Within moments, she realized that a rail fence, not a

picket fence, was what she needed in a field scene.

Nancy chose a dark sky for this quilt and made it extend only one quarter of the distance from top to bottom. That increased the sense that the sky was farther away, which in turn increased the sense of depth in the quilt.

osition the largest flowers in the foreground.

Only a small portion of the print above was used to make distant sunflowers.

Place medium-size flowers in the middle.

Nancy fussy-cut the sunflowers, starting with the smallest versions in the distance, and gradually increased their size as they approached the foreground.

Creating a Rail Fence

- Cut 3"-wide (or whatever width your design requires) strips from a wood-tone print. Using a rotary cutter, a ruler, and a mat, cut each strip so the grain of the fabric is vertical in the strip.
- To create each rail post, fold lengthwise (long) edges of the fabric strip. Starting at the cut edge, cut down a slight curve to the fold (approximately ½") *(Diagram A)*. Open the strip.
- To make the rail post top, cut a 3" square. Fold the square in half, but this time fold it so that the wood grain is cross-wise. Cut an outward curve with the same amount of pitch (½") *(Diagram B)*. Open the strip.
- Tuck the outward curve under the fence post top until the "rounded" shape appears *(Diagram C)*. Glue it to the quilt top.

Double-Border Fabric Combination

The purpose of the borders on a landscape quilt is to add a tranquil frame. However, for this quilt, a single brown border was too dull. When Nancy auditioned the borders, the only logical additional color option was gold. Initially, the finished width of the inner border was ½". But when Nancy pinned up the quilt to study it before adding the backing and the batting, she realized that the gold inner border was overpowering. To soften the effect, she stitched a ¼" deeper seam allowance on the inner border, leaving the gold accent strip only ¼" wide. (See page 134 for quilting and page 136 for binding.)

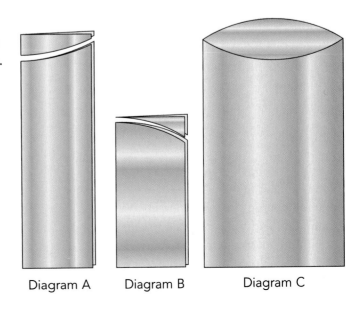

Diagram A   Diagram B   Diagram C

Creating *Poppies Out My Window*

Imagine looking out a window to catch a glimpse of a garden in full bloom. Designing a landscape quilt that mimics that vantage point offers another option for indoor fabric gardening. This quilt by Natalie Sewell does just that, highlighting the structural element of a window frame.

Poppies Out My Window by Natalie Sewell
(30" x 28")

 See "Cutting and Gluing Techniques" on page 20 before beginning.

Creating the Background

- Use a dark hand-dyed or batik fabric for the upper one-third sky portion of the background.
- Select a multicolored foliage print for the lower two-thirds of the background. Messy-cut the top edge of the foliage print. Apply glue to that edge and overlap the lower edge of the sky *(Photo A)*.

Adding Foreground Foliage

- Choose a variety of grasses and foliage to convey poppy leaves and grasses.
- Use fussy-cutting techniques to cut shapes.
- Glue and position the grasses and foliage in the foreground *(Photo B)*.

Note from Natalie: To expand your fabric choices, bleach one or more foliage prints to add highlights and to change the fabric's appearance. Make a solution of three parts water to one part bleach. Always test a small sample of the fabric before bleaching the entire piece. Every fabric is different, so not all bleach the same. Scrunch the fabric and place it in the solution for five minutes. If the results are not what you want, adjust the solution or the timing or use a different fabric. If you are happy with the results, soak the bleached fabric in clear water to stop the bleaching process.

Unbleached fabric

Bleached fabric

Adding the Poppies

- Use fabric paint or markers to intensify and highlight the color of the poppies. Color the poppies first; then cut them out.
- Cut some of the poppy shapes smaller to obtain a wide variety of poppies in various sizes.
- Create oval-shaped buds from green batik fabric.
- Cut stems from the same green batik fabric.
- Glue both buds and stems carefully (when thin and small, they have a tendency to break apart) with a glue stick and position them on the quilt top *(Photo C)*.

Adding Windowpane Dividers

- Select one or more wood-print fabrics. Use the lighter shades within the fabric for the wooden dividers that separate the individual panes. Use darker shades for the sash (the frame around the outside of the panes). Or if the fabric does not have distinctive shading, use fabric paints or markers to darken the sash.
- Cut the windowpane dividers, using a rotary cutter. The strips on the featured quilt are ½" wide.
- Position the strips on the quilt. Measuring is important to ensure that you space the window dividers evenly; it will be a crucial part of squaring up the quilt later on.
- Divide both the top and lower edges of the quilt into thirds. Mark these points for placement of the two vertical strips.
- Divide each side edge in half. Mark the placement for the horizontal strip.
- Apply glue to the back of the fabric strips. Position the strips on the quilt at the marked positions *(Photo D)*.

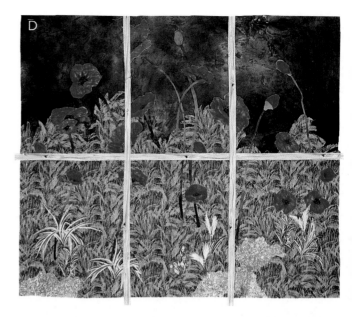

Adding the Window Frame Borders

- Machine-baste the cut pieces to the background and square the quilt top.

 See *"Machine-Stitching the Quilt Top" on page 21 before beginning.*

 See *"Squaring the Quilt Top" on page 23 before beginning.*

 See *"Adding Borders" on page 24 before beginning.*

Note from Nancy: The window frame is crucial to this design, but the frame is really your quilt's border. Therefore, you will need to machine-baste your quilt top and square it up before you add the window-frame border.

- Add borders, using the same fabric as the windowpane dividers. Cut your border strips 2" wide, giving you a finished border of 1½".
- Watch the direction of the wood grain to make sure it runs vertically at the sides and horizontally at the top and the bottom of the window.
- See page 134 for quilting and page 136 for binding your quilt.

Creating *Alaine's Window*

*Position window frame fabrics differently to create the look of an open
window. In this instance, having a photo for reference proved invaluable.*

A professional photo inspired *Alaine's Window*. The
photographer, Alaine Johnson, of Stoughton,
Wisconsin, placed an old window in the midst of a garden
bed. The result is charming, partly because it doesn't make
visual sense. Natalie decided logic didn't matter for her either
when she re-created the same scene in fabric.

To make the window look slightly ajar, the top panes need to

swerve down slightly to the left, and the bottom panes need to
swerve up slightly to the left. Natalie shaded the window frame
with a white fabric marker to make it look as if the sun was hitting
it. She used an unrelated pale blue border and let some of the
flowers protrude onto it, again not worrying about logic or reality.
As for the flowers and the background, Natalie used the techniques
described in "Creating *White Picket Fence*," pages 46–49.

Alaine's Window by Natalie Sewell (42" x 54")

Three Grapevine Quilts

*Latticework and vines created from bias trim are lovely enhancements
for landscape quilts. Natalie used them to create the look of stained glass.*

***The Grapevine* by Natalie Sewell (36" x 27")**

This quilt uses hand-dyed fabric in every section except the leaves and the grapes, which come from a commercial fabric. The hand-dyes give the sense that the scene is dappled with sunlight and shade. The vines are a shade of dark gray; the latticework (here a simple rectangle) is made from the same fabric as the border. The vines are handmade bias trim.

View from the Grape Arbor by Natalie Sewell
(40" x 46")

For this quilt, Natalie first created a simple scene—water and sky—with a mountain range in between. All the fabrics are hand-dyed. The lattice-work in this quilt is a simple series of double overlapping bars, handmade by the method described on pages 60 and 61, and are hand-appliquéd to the background fabric. The vines are bias trim, handmade from a brown batik. To intensify the stained-glass look in the grapes and the leaves, Natalie outlined them with fabric paint markers. She used dark green for the leaves and dark gray for the grapes.

The Grapevine Panel by Natalie Sewell
(20" x 46")

This quilt offers a third design option for a scene with latticework and vines. Natalie used the techniques for handmade bias trim outlined on pages 60 and 61 to make the lattice and the vines.

Lattice Accents

Latticework, varying in width from 1" to 2", can be created exactly the same way as windowpane dividers (page 56). Cut straight strips of fabric and attach them by machine, stitching directly to the background fabric. Like all of the other design elements in the quilt, the edges are unfinished.

Another way to create latticework is to make 1"-wide (or wider) bias trim from strips that have finished edges. Refer to the instructions below for creating custom-made bias trim. If your latticework does not curve, you can cut your strips on the straight of the grain.

Vine Accents

Vines, only ¼" wide, need to swirl and sway across your quilt—a motion achieved only by using the bias of the fabric.

There are two kinds of bias trim: the kind you make yourself out of whatever fabric you choose to use, and the kind you buy ready made. The advantage of the first kind is that you can use marbled, mottled fabric with areas of light and dark. The disadvantage is that they require more work and time, and you will have to position them on the quilt top with hand or machine basting.

Note from Natalie: Handwork may seem a disadvantage to some, but it is an advantage to me. I love hand appliquéing, and landscape quilting affords very few opportunities for handwork. I think I designed these vine and latticework quilts just to give me a chance to hand appliqué. They are great projects to work on while traveling.

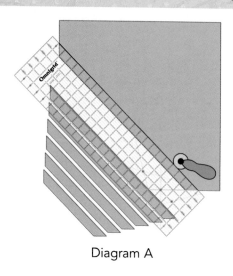

Diagram A

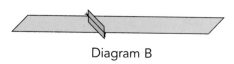

Diagram B

Custom-Made Bias Option

To make your own bias trim, select an appropriate fabric. Use variegated light and dark brown batiks to create vines for grape arbors or vining flowers, such as wisteria or clematis. Since the seam is hidden underneath the bias strip, you will avoid the frustration of having to turn under a seam allowance as you sew.

You will need **plastic or metal bias bars** of varying widths, which you can purchase at most fabric or quilting shops or from catalogs. The suggested finished width is ¼" for vines.

- To cut true bias, align the bottom of your fabric with the 45º angle line on your rotary-cutting ruler. Cut 1"-wide parallel strips (*Diagram A*). Or fold the fabric diagonally and press a crease line, and then cut parallel to the fold.
- Join strips into 1 piece with a diagonal seam (*Diagram B*).
- Fold the strips in half lengthwise, with the wrong sides together. Stitch along the cut edges with a ¼" seam. Trim the seam allowance to ⅛", as shown in foreground of *Photo A*.
- Insert a plastic or metal bias bar into the bias tube, with the seam running down the center of one flat side of the bar. Press the tubing flat with a hot DRY iron (*Photo A*). Move the rod down the length of the tubing and press the entire tube flat. Be careful when handling the hot bar; let it cool for a few seconds before moving it down the tube. Remove the bias tube, and you are ready to pin the vine in place. *Do not turn the tube.* When stitching in place, lay the exposed seam next to the quilt.

Note from Nancy: When using bias bars, stitch a test seam allowance and insert a bar in the tube to make certain that the seam allowance is not too tight or too loose. Adjust the seam width if necessary.

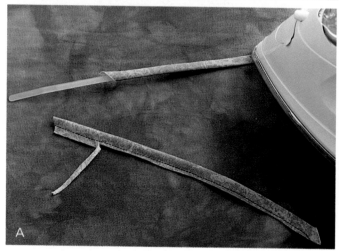

A

Use bias bars to press the seam to the middle, where it will be hidden when stitched in place.

- Using large basting stitches on your sewing machine (or by hand), baste the vine onto your quilt background and latticework frame. You may want to pull it under and over the structure of the latticework. As you add vines to your scene, hide the ends by tucking them under the lattice *(Photo B)*.
- Position and glue leaves, flowers, and grapes, hiding the ends of the vines with some of these. Hand-appliqué both sides of all exposed areas of the vine. Remove the basting.

Quick Bias Option

You can purchase premade ¼"-wide bias strips in a variety of solid colors. The backs of these strips are bonded with a paper-backed fusible web *(Photo C)*. Simply remove the paper backing and press them into place on your quilt background *(Photo D)*. Since they are cut on the bias, they will twist and turn smoothly to make vines. They must be secured with hand stitching, as mentioned above. The webbing is provided for positioning only, not permanent bonding. This option is a quick and effective method of creating latticework and vines. The disadvantage is that you are restricted to solid colors and have a limited color selection.

B

C

Quick fusible bias is available in solid colors. It is a speedy alternative for creating latticework and vines.

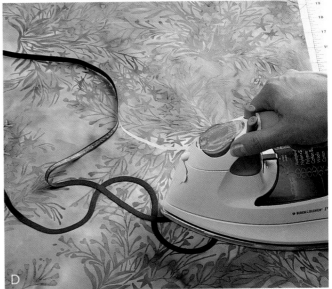

D

Simply remove the paper backing, position the bias on the fabric, and fuse it in place.

Creating Still-Life Flower Quilts

Still life has been a popular art form for centuries and is just as available to the quilter as it is to the oil painter. The inspiration for the two still-life quilts featured here are two impressionist artists, Claude Monet and Pierre Bonnard. Making an indoor still-life quilt will give you a new perspective on using printed fabric to create walls, tables, and vases, as well as flowers and leaves.

Monet's Sunflowers by Natalie Sewell (34" x 40")

The first challenge in recreating Monet's *Sunflowers* was to find fabrics that would convey the heavy brushstrokes and hues of the walls and the table. Natalie found a commercial batik for the walls. For the table and the border, she chose a piece of red hand-dyed fabric that conveyed the multitoned painted effect she needed. The vase is made from a piece of cream-colored muslin.

The flowers and the leaves posed a bigger problem. Her sunflower fabric had a variety of sizes of flowers, but they had pale centers and were all facing forward. As often happens, the leaves on the sunflower print were too small and too few. In addition, the background was bright red.

Natalie darkened the centers, using black and brown fabric markers, as

shown in the photo above. Next, she cut the flowers out very carefully, making sure she removed any trace of the red background. Then she turned the flowers in different directions by cutting some of them apart and moving the petals in different directions.

Natalie found two leaf fabrics to use—one light for the top of the bouquet and one darker for the bottom.

Natalie enhanced the colors of the flower petals by adding a few strokes with her red fabric marker.

Bonnard's Poppies by Natalie Sewell (33" x 40")

For this quilt, Natalie chose hand-dyed light gray fabric (by Sharon Luehring) for the background and two commercial batiks for the green panel on the left and for the table. She cut the yellow panel from Mickey Lawler's Skydye fabric. She stitched the wall pieces together at the top two-thirds of the quilt and then cut and glued the table to the bottom third. She then drew a free-form vase on a piece of commercial white fabric with a mottled hue and added gray marks to the vase with a gray marker.

Natalie gave herself free rein in choosing flower fabrics. She cut out some big red roses and gave them black centers with a fabric marker. She enhanced the petals with a red fabric marker. The clustered blossoms, both cream and light blue, were cut from a piece of upholstery fabric. The leaves were cut freehand with scissors from green batik. Natalie tried to capture the "weedy" look of Bonnard's flowers by giving them long, angular stems and letting a few flowers and leaves hang down against the vase as if they were broken.

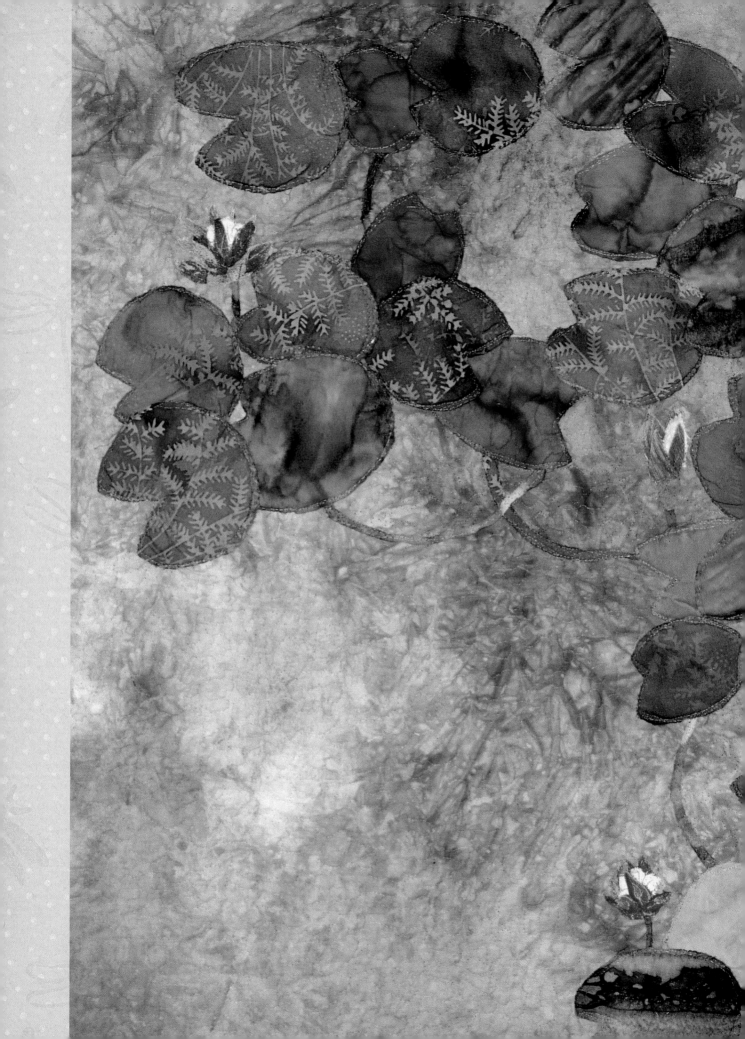

4

Cutting
Free-form Shapes

When you can't find just the right
floral or leaf print, knowing how to
cut free-form shapes can be very
helpful. Flowers and leaves cut from
batiks or hand-dyed fabrics can
create an impressionistic look not
possible with motifs cut from floral
prints. At times, that may be just
what you want.

Water Lilies **by Nancy Zieman**
(31" x 48")

Creating *Water Lilies*

Impressionism was exactly what Nancy Zieman was going for when she created this quilt. Discover how she did it below.

Getting Started

Start with a good photo or drawing. The inspiration for *Water Lilies* came from a note-card photo (shown below) entitled *The Last Lily of Summer*, taken by outdoor photographers Ken and Doris Zeyher of Beaver Dam, Wisconsin. Remember that you can interpret your photo freely, as Nancy did. Study the leaves and the petals on the flowers. Then start cutting the same shapes from the fabric of your choice. Expect to throw away some of your first tries.

The beauty of nature is that no two flowers are exactly alike. That's why Nancy didn't make a template for her flower petals. She cut them free-form, so each flower or leaf is slightly different from the others.

Choosing Fabrics

For the water, Nancy selected a hand-dyed fabric in shades of blue and tan to represent shadows from trees and clouds.

To create the lily pads, she needed a variety of different fabrics. She couldn't find any that depicted lily pads in the size and coloration she wanted, so she cut them free-form from eight batiks and batiklike fabrics that ranged from blue-green to olive green, gold, and brown.

Nancy used a fall leaf print to make the flowers in the top portion of the quilt and a large tropical print for the flowers in the lower two-thirds. The designs in these fabrics were not critical; rather, they were chosen for the coloration within the print.

Hand-dyed fabrics and batiks work well in landscape quilts.

Choose blues for a few lily pads.

Select a variety of green batiks for the lily pads.

For realism, use at least one gold or brown fabric for dead leaves.

You may find landscape elements in unexpected fabrics. Nancy used both the tropical print at right and the fall leaf print at far right to make flowers.

See "Cutting and Gluing" on page 20 before continuing.

Cutting Freeform Flowers and Leaves

- From your lily-pad fabrics, cut oval shapes in a variety of sizes, with indentations to simulate lily-pad leaves *(Photo A)*.
- Cut vines from darker leaf fabrics. Since the vines are underwater, they appear darker than the leaves.
- Cut the lilies' petal shapes from a print fabric *(Photo B)*. Frequently, water lilies have yellow centers. Consider adding a touch of yellow for brightness and realism, either by cutting out a yellow fabric center or by highlighting the center with a yellow fabric marker *(Photo B)*.

Laying Out the Quilt

- Look carefully at the light and dark sections of your background fabric. Place your darker leaves in the sections of the pond that are darkest.
- Use a combination of several leaf colors to represent the different ages of the leaves.
- Glue the leaves in place. Also glue the slightly curved stems between leaves so that they appear as if they are growing underwater *(Photo C)*.

Note from Nancy: The lily pads on the note card did not have stems, but I added them, since I frequently see the stems when I look at lily pads in other pictures or when I see them along the edge of a lake or a pond.

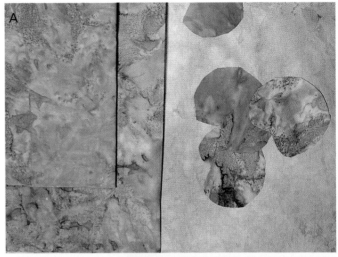

• Place and glue water lilies randomly on the quilt, remembering to use different shades of flowers to coincide with light and dark sections of the background *(Photos D and E)*. Tuck the edges of some lily pads under others.

 See *"Machine-Stitching the Quilt Top"* on page 21 for more information.

 See *"Squaring the Quilt Top"* on page 23 for more information.

Adding Borders

 See *"Adding Borders"* on page 24 before continuing.

Water Lilies has a 1"-wide inner border of olive green to give some tranquillity to the piece and an outer border of the same fabric as the background to give the quilt the impression of a continuing pond.

D

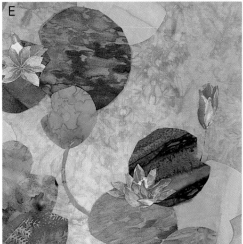

E

Repeating the background fabric in the outer border enhances the impression of a pond; the thin inner border adds tranquility to the piece.

Creating *Irises in My Garden*

*For this quilt, Nancy broke the rule of using a greeting
card or a photo for inspiration. Instead, she chose to replicate the irises
that were growing in her own garden at home.*

***Irises in My Garden* by Nancy Zieman (40" x 34")**

Choosing Fabrics

For the mauve irises in her rock garden, Nancy chose a batik with many shades, from yellow to mauve to burgundy, and selected five small-scale leaf and floral fabrics to surround her irises.

Creating the Blossoms

- Study a garden catalog or a photo of an iris before cutting out shapes. Irises have two main parts, so cut the upper and lower petals separately *(Photo A)*.
- Cut teardrop shapes for buds. Add a small green fabric base to the bud to simulate an iris bud.
- Create depth by making the irises in the background much smaller in scale than the flowers in the foreground.
- Add touches of color to the foreground foliage by messy-cutting abstract flowers *(Photo B)*.

Note from Nancy: The tiny yellow flowers in this quilt were cut from a remnant of decorating fabric. Unlike cottons, this loosely woven fabric ravels if you look at it the wrong way! To minimize the raveling, I quilted only the centers—not the edges—and sealed the edges with Fray Check®.

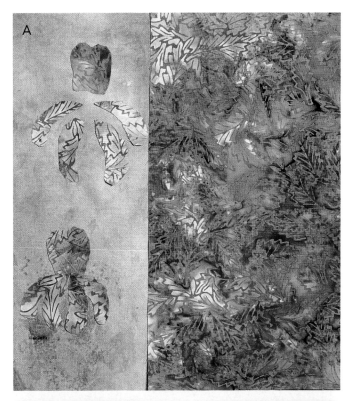

Creating *Trillium*

*A photo that Nancy took in the woods one spring
inspired Natalie to make this quilt. The brown leaves behind the brilliant white
and green flowers suggest that winter has just barely faded.*

Trillium by Natalie Sewell (42" x 34")

Instead of the green background of Nancy's photo, Natalie used a hand-dyed piece that she had just purchased. "The fabric suggested to me the color of the earth before spring emerges," says Natalie. "Nancy's photo was invaluable for making the blossoms and leaves and suggesting the nature of a clump of trillium."

Choosing Fabric

In addition to a beige/mauve hand-dyed fabric for the background, Natalie picked an assortment of brown and dark purple leaves that would look like old oak leaves in various stages of decay. The dark tree trunk contrasts with the brightness of the trillium.

Creating the Blossoms

- Trillium are complicated flowers at first glance, but they can be created easily in stages. The three white petals have slightly ruffled edges and are a similar shape to the leaf. Cut the petals from a piece of snow white fabric and the leaves from a piece of green batik. Cut both petals and leaves freehand to give each a unique shape *(Photo A)*.
- Cut a very small stamen from yellow cotton for each flower. Rub a glue stick on the center of each flower; then carefully attach a stamen to each flower with tweezers.
- Slightly darken the center of each petal with a gray fabric marker to give it depth *(Photo B)*.
- Trillium have a series of light green small leaves under each blossom. Use light green fabric to cut the leaves. Draw veins with a gray fabric marker.
- Glue the trillium petals and leaves together and then glue them to the background fabric *(Photo B)*.
- Create twigs and branches around the clump of trillium by using small pieces of dark fabric and machine embroidery, with black thread in both the bobbin and the needle. *(Photo C)*. For more information on machine embroidery, see "Machine Embroidery Techniques" on page 128.

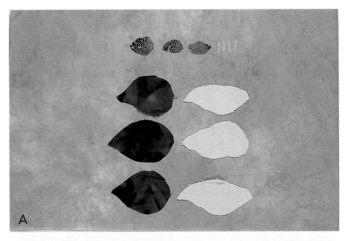

A

B

C

Creating *Wisteria*

Batiks and hand-dyed fabrics can convey a stained-glass look. Combining these fabrics with dark bias vines re-creates the effect of stained glass.

Creating *Wisteria*

*Natalie began designing this quilt on a long plane trip to
visit her sister. She had no inspirational photo and no idea where the design
was going—just a bag of fabric and a memory of Tiffany's stained glass.*

***Wisteria* by Natalie Sewell (48" x 44")**

Choosing Fabric

The inspiration for this landscape quilt was Tiffany's stained-glass collection at the Metropolitan Museum of Art in New York. Natalie chose a hand-dyed background fabric with shades of pink, light blue, and green—a fabric that had similar characteristics to the stained glass she saw at the museum.

For the blossoms and leaves, Natalie chose commercial batiks. She used purple and blue shades for the wisteria blossoms and a variety of greens for the leaves.

Creating the Blossoms and Leaves

- Draw long, slender, bumpy shapes freehand on various shades of purple batiks and cut them out *(Photo B)*. Use a variety of shades for realism.
- Cut a variety of leaf shapes. Notice in *Photo A* that light to dark colorations were combined within the same leaf clusters.
- Outline the leaf shapes with a black fabric marker, giving the leaves definition and the leaded look of stained glass.

Note from Natalie: I designed this landscape quilt cross-country, starting in Wisconsin and finishing in California. I hand-stitched the lattice and vines to the background fabric prior to a trip to visit my sister in Laguna Beach, California. I then began the process of drawing and cutting out the wisteria blossoms on the plane.

Once at my sister's home, I hung the background fabric on a banister (a make-shift design wall) and started gluing. I had lots of help from relatives, who all took turns placing blossoms and leaves on the quilt.

Every time I look at this quilt, I remember how much fun we had gluing and positioning the pieces. I still remember which blossoms my sister, Sheila, placed.

 See "Machine-Stitching the Quilt Top" on page 21 for more information.

 See "Squaring the Quilt Top" on page 23 for more information.

 See "Adding Borders" on page 24 for more information.

A

See page 60 for information on making vines.

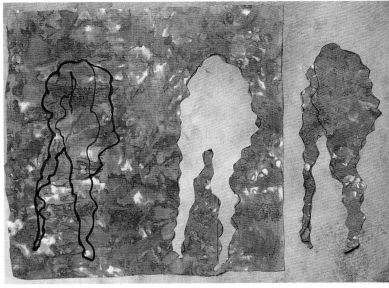

B

5

Creating Woodland Scenes

Now that you're familiar with the basic techniques of landscape quilting, you're ready to tackle a more challenging design concept: woodland scenes. In this chapter, you'll learn to design trees, backgrounds, and foregrounds from a more distant perspective. You'll be looking for a whole new range of photos to inspire you and for very different types of fabric. Creating trees requires stepping back far enough from your subject that the leaves appear as blurred brushstrokes instead of as veined individual objects; the same is true for ground cover and shrubs.

Kentucky Dogwoods by Natalie Sewell
(67" x 49")

Creating Distant Woodland Scenes

Choose a photo you love—one that is set during your favorite season, contains luscious colors, or evokes a sense of peace or joy. If it has a waterfall, reflecting pond, or other complicated element, put it aside for now. You'll want your first woodland scene to be simple. Pick something you can manage without having to enroll in an art class.

Getting Started

Sources for woodland scenes are everywhere: Greeting cards, calendars, postcards, and travel books are full of them, as are landscape photography books from your local library.

Just as you did with flower garden photos, you need to study the light in your woodland scene. What time of day is it? Where is the sun? Is it foggy or clear? Many woodland scenes have rays of sun penetrating the trees (see the photo below). As beautiful as that look is, avoid it for your first landscape. Those rays require special fabric or special bleaching and dying—all too much to deal with at first.

Does the photo you have fallen in love with have a misshapen tree or rock formation that you don't think you can reproduce? If so, leave it out. Just as with flower garden quilts, you're the artist. You can leave out anything you don't like or that seems too difficult. Conversely, you can add what you like. Feel free to combine elements from several photos to get what you consider to be the ideal scene.

From Photo to Fabric

A photo that inspires you is an important first step in developing your woodland scene.

The first time Natalie saw southern dogwood, she was on her first trip to the American Quilter's Society show in Paducah, Kentucky. The dogwood seemed to float in the air along the roadside as she drove south in April. When Natalie found a postcard in Kentucky that captured that floating quality, she made up her mind to re-create it in fabric.

As the photo at right illustrates, the range of color around the dogwood is limited—the gray and black of the trees, the green of the new leaves and foliage, and the snow white of the blossoms offer a limited pallette. The fabrics had to be just right to capture all of this.

As you can see in the quilt below, Natalie deviated considerably from the photo. Her quilt scene is horizontal,

although the photo is vertical and reveals much more of the gray sky. She added a few birch trees for texture and interest.

Natalie learned two important techniques from the photo: how to diminish the contrast of the trees in the distance and how to make the dogwood branches stretch horizontally. The gray trees were just what Natalie needed to create depth, as you will see in detail when we re-create a similar quilt step-by-step starting on page 88. And placing the petals one by one was crucial to making them into dogwood blossoms.

Kentucky Dogwoods won first place in the theme category at the 2000 American Quilter's Society Show in Paducah, Kentucky.

***Kentucky Dogwoods* by Natalie Sewell (67" x 49")**

Poppies Under the Olive Tree by Natalie Sewell (48" x 40")

On a spring trip to Israel, Natalie was enchanted by the many uncultivated fields of wildflowers that she saw, especially the poppy fields. Here and there among the fields stood ancient olive trees. Natalie felt the scenes were just waiting to be combined in a landscape quilt.

A postcard Natalie found in a Jerusalem gift shop became her inspirational photo (at right). The view is from the perspective of a picnicker gazing at the tree while sitting among the poppies.

Natalie chose a more dramatic fabric for her sky than the sky in the postcard suggests. She spent hours working on the olive tree, cutting dozens of spiked leaves and struggling to capture the movement in the photo.

This quilt became Natalie's husband's favorite.

The brilliant red of a neighbor's Japanese maple, shown in the photo at left, inspired *Dancing Maples*, shown below. Natalie was intrigued not only by the fall color, but also by the shape of the branches.

Natalie also loved the gold leaves on the branches extending above the maple in the photo, so she repeated it in the shrubs and the ground cover below her trees. In addition, she removed all architecture from the scene and used a background fabric that looks as if the woods go on forever.

Dancing Maples was juried into Visions: Quilt Expressions, sponsored by Quilt San Diego, in 1998.

***Dancing Maples* by Natalie Sewell (63" x 42")**

Creating *Autumn*

The quilt shown below may be simple, but it contains all the components of a much more complicated distant woodland scene. If you can re-create the simple design shown, you are well on your way to making more elaborate landscapes. For this reason, we have given step-by-step instructions for making it.

Autumn by Natalie Sewell (28" x 24")

Getting Started

Natalie had only to open her front door one golden October for the inspiration for this quilt. The Japanese maple wasn't in the scene she saw; she put it there to add a touch of red. She combined elements of both of the photos shown here.

Choosing Fabrics

Choose a multishaded fabric with mottled hues—either commercial or hand-dyed—for your background fabric. Audition a background fabric by pinning it to your design wall and then stepping back to view it from a distance. If portions of the fabric seem to blend into one another and become one solid mass, pick something else. Avoid fabrics that have only one or two hues. From a distance, they will appear as solids.

The best background fabrics for distant woodland scenes will make your job easier, not harder, by appearing to have clumps of leaves already visible in the distance and patches of sky peeking through clouds.

Hand-dyed fabrics make excellent background fabrics for woodland scenes. Their clumps, blotches, and scrunched areas naturally mimic branches, trees and glimpses of sky. Overdying only enriches their natural look.

Some commercial fabrics are also excellent choices. Select an irregular design of ferns or leaves or perhaps a motif from nature. Fabrics with geometric motifs won't work, no matter how beautiful they are. You'll waste energy and time trying to cover up the unnatural elements.

The background fabric Natalie used for *Autumn* is a commercial mauve batik with irregular shrublike markings and at least four or five different hues ranging from gray to peach.

You will need at least two different leaf fabrics and four or five kinds of ground cover fabric. Watch your scale here. The foliage for both leaves and ground cover needs to be small and indistinct in order to convey distance. Natalie used golds and grays, as well as rusts and browns. She added a green for the evergreen shrubs.

Note from Natalie: You can double your fabric choices by using both right and wrong sides of the fabric.

Look for a bright red brush-marked fabric to use as your focal point: the Japanese maple tree. If you can't find a bright red, you can always enhance the color of a chosen fabric with fabric paint or markers.

For the tree trunks, select two wood-grain prints. Choose a lighter shade for the background trees and darker shades for the foreground trees, thus reinforcing the feeling of depth or perspective. Use both right and wrong sides of the fabrics for greater variation and realism.

Use a dark wood-grain print for trees in the foreground and a lighter print for distant trees.

Pick one bright red print for the maple tree.

This fabric is an excellent choice for shrubs.

Small, indistinct prints work well for ground cover and leaves.

Adding Background Foliage, Leaves, and Tree Trunks

 See "Cutting and Gluing" on page 20 before continuing.

- Cut a 24" x 18" rectangle from your background fabric.
- Pin the background fabric to your design wall. (See page 26 for information on creating a vertical design wall.)
- Using your foliage fabrics, messy-cut leaf sections, using right and wrong sides of the fabric to create an abundance of leaves clustered together.
- Position and glue the shapes randomly side by side along the top third of the quilt.
- Cut out the tree trunks, using a rotary cutter and a mat but no ruler *(Photo A)*. Cut the tree shapes with natural curves and uneven shaping, making the trunks fatter at the bottom. Avoid straight, telephone pole shapes. Let the trunks curve and sway. Round the base of the trunk for realism. Glue the trees in place *(Photo B)*.

Adding Shrubs, Ground Cover, and Foreground Trees *(Photo C)*

- Cut the foreground trees from the darker wood-grain fabric. Create narrow branches, using scissors. Branches need bumps and elbows to look realistic. Angle-cut the branch ends and glue the trees to the background fabrics.

Note from Natalie: Some of my best branches have come from my sewing room floor. Here's an instance where scraps can come in handy!

- Messy-cut the ground cover shapes. Ground cover tends to grow in elongated half-moon shapes.
- Glue the pieces to the quilt. Stand back and look at the design. If you're dissatisfied, reglue the pieces in more effective spots.
- Create depth by placing the darker colors in the foreground.
- Give the illusion of the sun coming through the trees by adding light sections in the background.

Adding Foreground Leaves and Shrubs *(Photo D)*
- Add the darker ground and leaf colors in the foreground.
- Position some shrubbery to cover the tree trunks; tuck other shrubs underneath the trunks.
- Allow some of the background fabric to show through the foreground.

Adding a Focal Point *(Photo E)*
- Add a touch of green; even in fall, there are still bits of green in nature.
- Position the Japanese maple trunk so that it is slightly off-center. Curve the tree trunk and its branches.
- Cut the leaves for the Japanese maple in horizontal sections.

 See "Machine Stitching the Quilt Top" on page 21 for more information.

 See "Squaring Up the Quilt Top" on page 23 for more information.

Auditioning Borders *(Photo F)*
The photo shows us auditioning two fabrics for borders. We chose a darker border for *Autumn,* but any one of several hues would work well here. Once you've made your selection, it's time to add the borders.

 See "Adding the Borders" on page 24 for more information.

Creating *Two Dogwoods*

Natalie designed the quilt shown below, which has about half the number of trees as our larger woodland scene quilts, to give you a more manageable experience. Once you learn to make this quilt, you will be able to create a larger version on your own.

Two Dogwoods **by Natalie Sewell (37" x 37")**

Choosing Fabrics

Although the following tips are geared for making *Two Dogwoods*, they are also helpful for making any distant woodland scene.

Note from Natalie: Fabric selection is without a doubt the key element in determining the success of any landscape quilt. The more detailed the design, the more specific the fabric selection.

Background Fabric

Choose a background fabric with subtle, mottled hues that are unevenly spread. For *Two Dogwoods*, we chose a greenish gray hand-dyed fabric. Cut a rectangle from your background fabric in any size desired.

Foliage Fabric

You will need at least two kinds of foliage fabrics: one for ground cover and the other for leaves. Both kinds need to have at least five different green hues to convey a natural look from a distance.

Two Dogwoods uses four ground cover fabrics: light silver-lavender with ferns, dark shrubbery, lighter grasses or moss, and yellow grasses or plants. Notice the light silver-lavender ground cover near the base of the birch trees in the photo on the opposite page. This fabric emphasizes the sky breaking through the trees. Don't forget that the underside of the fabric offers a sunlight effect wherever you need it.

You will need at least two kinds of leaf fabric for your trees. The first kind should be just a shade or two different from the color of the background. By messy-cutting it very small and placing it on the most distant trees, you can create depth and texture for your scene. The second should be a small-scale distinct leaf fabric with at least five shades of green—some dark, some light—and with a good reverse side that can provide a sun-dappled look.

Tree Trunk Fabrics

Choose at least four different tree trunk fabrics: birch, medium gray, dark gray, and black. Place the lightest tree trunks farthest away from the foreground and add increasingly darker tree trunks as you move forward in your scene. The distant trees will look slightly obscured by fog, again creating a sense of depth.

Make sure you have enough fabric for plenty of trees and branches. There are approximately 20 trees in this quilt—and even though you don't have to make that many, you need enough to create the look of woods stretching back into the distance.

Floral Fabric

The only floral fabric needed—unless you want to add wildflowers to the forest floor—is for the dogwood blossoms. Since the blossoms are tiny and distant, simple stark white muslin works well. Don't use a cream color; it won't stand out.

Use a variety of foliage fabrics for ground cover and leaves.

Pick one floral fabric for the dogwood blossoms.

Use dark gray and black prints for tree trunks.

Creating Distant Ground Cover and Leaves *(Photo A)*

- Pin the background fabric to a design wall.
- Messy-cut distant ground cover and leaves from fabrics that are most similar in color to your background fabric. Glue the ground cover at least a third of the way up from the bottom of the background fabric and glue the leaves near the top of the background fabric. The farther down on the background fabric the leaves come in the scene and the farther up the ground cover, the greater the sense of depth you will create in the scene.

See "Cutting and Gluing" on page 20 before continuing

Note from Natalie: To make distant woodland scenes, you will need to fine-tune your messy-cutting techniques. When viewed from a distance, leaves and ground cover should look more like variegated dot patterns or brushstrokes. They should form irregular clumps with jagged edges. Cut rough, jagged shapes to denote distant shrubs and leaf clumps. Avoid cutting cloud or lollipop shapes; nature rarely has smooth edges.

Creating Distant Trees *(Photo B)*

- Choose the lightest shade from your tree trunk fabrics for your background trees. (You may use both right and wrong sides of the fabric to create the effect of sunlight.) These will be your smallest tree trunks. Cut them using a rotary cutter without a ruler. Fold the fabric in half and cut two trees at one time. (See tree trunk cutting techniques on page 86.)
- Apply glue to the side of fabric you are not displaying. (It may not always be the wrong side.) Position the trunks at different intervals on the background fabric, starting with the farthest trees about a third of the way up the background. Later, the foreground trees will be nearer the lower edges of the background fabric.
- Your tree trunks need not be a single piece. Once the landscape scene is finished and quilted, no one will be able to tell that you've overlapped pieces with glue to make a single tree trunk.
- Place some portions of the tree trunks behind the leaf shapes or other foliage. Position the trees so that they sometimes cross each other or twist. Sway each one slightly.

Note from Natalie: One side of each tree will be slightly shaded. Wait to highlight this with fabric paint until later in the process, because you will be covering sections of tree trunks with leaves and other branches.

Creating the Middle Ground *(Photo C)*

- Add more leaves, ground cover, and trees, choosing fabrics from the middle range of your fabric hues. Messy-cut leaves to ensure natural shapes. Position the leaves lower than those in the distance and have a few cover the tops of the distant tree trunks.
- Add to your ground cover, extending it to the bottom of the quilt. Add sun-drenched shrubbery and leaves. You may paint these prior to cutting by simply coloring over the fabric with a yellow fabric marker.
- After completing the ground cover, add medium gray trees. Place the trees slightly lower on the background than the lightest trees. Remember to round the bottom of the tree trunks.
- Step back occasionally to see if you're achieving the results you desire. View the quilt from a distance of at least 20 feet if you can; or look at the scene through a camera lens. Change or rearrange sections until you're pleased with the results. You should start to see areas of light and dark in your woods. Let your background fabric dictate where the lightest sections are by placing them in the lightest part of the fabric.

Adding the Foreground *(Photo D)*

- Add your darkest, biggest trees to the foreground. Place your tree trunks even lower on the quilt top, perhaps only a few inches from the bottom. But be careful to stagger them; you don't want them standing in a row.
- Add more leaves to hide some of the treetops in the middle ground.
- Fussy-cut some golden foliage pieces for the foreground. Glue them on, scattered over the ground cover.

Shading the Tree Trunks with Fabric Paint *(Photo E)*

- Look carefully at your scene and decide where your light source is coming from—the right or the left. Let your background fabric guide you. If you can't tell, just pick one.
- If the light source is coming from the left, shade the right sides of the trees with a black or gray fabric marker. If the trees are black, use a white or light gray marker on the same side as the light source. While you have your markers handy, use them to add texture, knot holes, or bark to your tree trunks. You can also add little branches between the trees and little twigs here and there.
- If any of your tree trunks are birch, add dark horizontal lines and marks on the white bark.

Note from Natalie: Shading the tree trunks gives them dimension. Until you paint the trunks of the trees, your scene will look flat and two-dimensional; once you shade them, your design will come alive.

Adding the Focal Point: The Dogwoods

- Cut skinny tree trunks on the bias from black fabric. Bias-cutting lets you bend and sway the trunks as you place them on the landscape scene. Add branches.
- Cut lots of tiny dogwood blossoms in oval shapes from your snow white fabric, using sharp embroidery scissors. Position the blossoms on the dogwood trees in horizontal rows. A good—but messy—way to do this is to stroke the quilt top in horizontal rows with your glue stick; then place the blossoms one by one on the sticky fabric. Use tweezers or your fingers.

Finishing Your Landscape Quilt

 See *"Machine-Stitching the Quilt Top"* on page 21 for more information.

 See *"Squaring Up the Quilt Top"* on page 23 for more information.

 See *"Adding Borders"* on page 24 for more information.

Natalie used tweezers to place the dogwood blossoms.

Showcase of Distant Woodland Scenes

The quilts shown here use the techniques learned in this chapter.

***Spring in the Woods* by Natalie Sewell (48" x 42")**

For this quilt, Natalie used a commercial batik for a background fabric. The commercial batik gave her a running start on her design by simulating trees, shrubs, and leaves in the distance even before any other fabrics were added.

Since the season is spring, the leaves on these slender trees are chartreuse and very small. To simulate tiny redbud blossoms, Natalie messy-cut a pink batik and scattered the pieces around the top half of the quilt.

The focus in this quilt is the ground cover. Natalie set the foreground abloom with spring wildflowers, especially trillium, which she cut from the same white fabric she used for the dogwood blossoms in *Two Dogwoods* on page 88. This time, however, she made clover-shaped blossoms, with three connecting petals. The yellow shrubs could be forsythia. Natalie says you should try not to worry about botanical accuracy, as long as you convey a spring feeling in the colors and the shapes.

*A*spens in Autumn is one of Nancy's first landscape quilts, completed shortly after working with Natalie on their first TV series. Inspiration came from a photo found in a woman's clothing catalog that featured a field of aspens in fall.

The background fabric is a navy-and-gold batik. To eliminate some busyness in the middle ground, Nancy cut out extra navy sections from her leftover batik to cover the gold parts and then added extra gold sections to the top of the quilt. The effect of the dark middle ground not only quieted the scene, but also gave it depth.

Nancy added dark trees over the navy background and used her lightest trees in the foreground. To get the foremost trees as light as possible, she used the wrong side of the fabric.

Aspens in Autumn **by Nancy Zieman (37" x 28")**

***Morning Mist* by Nancy Zieman (48" x 39")**

The inspiration for this quilt came from a child's book on redwoods that Nancy and her youngest son, Tom, were reading; the blotches of color on the background fabric became small distant trees, with the aid of machine embroidery. Purple leaves and background hills in shades of purple added depth and color. Nancy repeated the purple in the hand-dyed inner border and let her foreground extend into the border.

$\mathcal{S}$omething wonderful happens to nature when the moon is bright. The whites become iridescent and all the foliage changes hue.

For this moonlit scene, Natalie used teal and purple with a few pale greens in the leaves. The background fabric is teal, which ranges from light to dark. It gives a dramatic effect but has no texture or mottling. So Natalie had a big job of messy-cutting and gluing background leaves and foliage to set the stage for the hydrangea trees.

The hydrangea blossoms are made from two fabrics, a pale, creamy flower print, covered partially with a snow white, messy-cut piece of fabric in the foreground. The white gives a moonlit glow to the hydrangeas. The border echoes the background fabric and the movement of the moonlight along the top of the scene.

Hydrangea Trees in Moonlight by Natalie Sewell (49" x 41")

This quilt has a very close foreground (the dark area) and a very distant background, making it particularly challenging. Don't choose this type of design if you're a first-time landscape quilter.

To make it even more challenging, Natalie didn't use a photo, and she'd never been to Appalachia. The quilt got its name because a friend who saw it said, "Oh, my gosh, it's exactly the spot where my husband and I picnicked when we toured the Appalachian Mountains last summer!"

Natalie's goal was to provide as great a contrast in light as she could. To get the yellow tones, she soaked green fabrics in bleach for a few minutes until she had the shade she wanted.

After she had glued down all her trees, Natalie decided that the quilt needed a brook. She couldn't bear to rip up the trees, so she cut the brook in pieces and fitted them between the foreground trees. She says she learned an important lesson: Landscape quilts are never done; you can always add something new to your scene.

Appalachian Summer by Natalie Sewell (67" x 49")

Creating Close-up Woodland Scenes

Not all woodland scenes are distant. Close-up woodland scenes give you a chance to show off beautiful leaves and branches. Following are step-by-step instructions for making Natalie's *Gray Day in August.*

Gray Day in August by Natalie Sewell (62" x 41")

Choosing Fabrics

This quilt has the same background fabric as *Kentucky Dogwoods* (page 78), a mottled hand-dyed fabric. But because the scene is so much closer and the season is different, the rest of the fabrics are different.

Select three leaf fabrics: light, medium, and dark. All three should be similar in scale and detailed enough to show veining. Choose one distant foliage fabric. A green works well. You will not need ground cover fabric, since the ground isn't visible.

Because the trees are so close to the viewer, you will need realistic tree trunk textures. Choose three tree trunk fabrics: light gray, medium gray or brown, and dark brown. All three should have barklike markings.

Choose one light, one medium, and one dark leaf fabric.

Select one light green for distant foliage.

Choose three shades for tree trunks to create depth.

Note from Natalie: Paint over the leaf fabrics with a yellow fabric marker to change their tone from green to yellow-green and dab all the fabric leaves with an orange fabric marker for a sun-kissed look.

Adding Background Trees and Foliage *(Photo A)*

 See "Cutting and Gluing Techniques" on page 20 before continuing.

- Cut a rectangle in the desired size from your background fabric. Pin it to the design wall.
- Choose the lightest and smallest-scale foliage. Messy-cut the background leaves. Position and glue them to the upper quarter of the quilt.
- Cut, glue, and position your palest tree trunks to the background fabric.

Adding the Middle-Range Trees and Foliage *(Photo B)*

- Cut, glue, and position your middle range gray tree trunks. Twist and turn them so they look natural.
- Fussy-cut the bottom shrubs. Add them to the bottom of the quilt over dark skinny shrub branches.

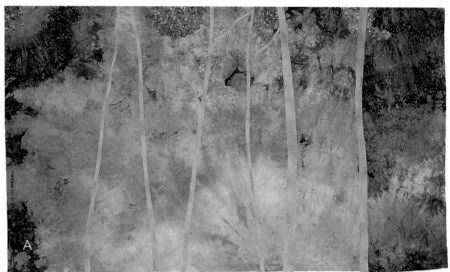

Creating the Foremost Tree Trunks *(Photo C)*

- Cut and add the brown tree trunks. Remember that because this is a close-up scene, the foremost tree trunks will be 2" to 3" inches wide. Tilt the trunks slightly; let the branches twist and turn.
- Add fussy-cut foliage in front of the middle range tree trunk tops. Add some foliage in front of the largest trees so that they will not control the scene.
- Cut two skinny sapling trunks and branches. Curve trunks and branches slightly.
- Paint the lightest colored leaves with yellow fabric markers and dab them with an orange marker here and there. Fussy-cut the leaves and glue them on the sapling branches.

Shading the Tree Trunks *(Photo D)*

- Review your scene to decide where the light is coming from. With a gray or black fabric marker, shade the side of each tree trunk away from the light source.
- Add pencil lines for small pale branches and paint extra knots on the tree trunks.
- If your tree trunks are very dark, you may want to add office "white out" chalk to the side of each tree closest to the light source.

Finishing Your Landscape Quilt

 See "Machine Stitching the Quilt Top" on page 21 for more information.

 See "Squaring Up the Quilt Top" on page 23 for more information.

Choosing the Border *(Photo E)*

A green border that picks up the colors of the quilt's foliage is effective. Try to avoid a dark brown border that might look like additional tree trunks. After you've added your border, glue more leaves onto your trees, extending them into the border.

 See "Adding Borders" on page 24 for more information.

Showcase of Close-up Woodland Scenes

The quilt at right features the scarlet colors of autumn. The background fabric, with its mottled hues of green, blue, and gray, hint at more woods in the distance without Natalie actually having to create distant foliage.

Natalie cut the three birch trees crosswise from a brown ragged-stripe fabric. Almost all of the bark markings were already in the fabric. She chose the green shrubbery at the bottom of the quilt because it so closely matched the background fabric itself and would strengthen the illusion of shrubs in the distance.

She created the branch of red maple leaves with two or three different red fabrics, a scattering of yellow fabric, and some red markers to intensify the color. Natalie chose not to use a border to give the quilt a contemporary look.

***Three Birches with Red Maple* by Natalie Sewell (39" x 29")**

***A.J.'s Autumn* by Natalie Sewell (45" x 38")**

Natalie made *A.J.'s Autumn* as a gift for her son, A.J. Natalie used a hand-dyed background fabric, cut 41" by 34", to begin this quilt.

Some of the trunks are green, creating a sense of moss and fungus in the woods. All the tree fabrics have good bark markings. Natalie enhanced this effect by shading them with fabric paint. The red leaves came from several red fabrics. Natalie worked carefully when positioning them to make sure that the darkest were buried inside the cluster of leaves and the lightest were placed on the outside of the clump of leaves to give a sun-kissed effect. Natalie chose a simple olive hand-dyed fabric for the border.

6

Creating Water, Sky, Mountains, and Snow

There is more to nature than trees and flowers. Eventually, you'll probably want to add water, sky, mountains, and snow to your landscape quilts. You'll find lots of exciting fabrics for such scenes.

In previous chapters, we urged you to choose photographs, calendars, and greeting cards to inspire you. Those make great inspirations in this chapter as well; but perhaps here, more than in any other chapter, the fabric itself can offer inspiration.

Golden Morning by Natalie Sewell
(39" x 35")

Capturing Details in Nature

Make good use of the specialty fabrics available to recreate details in nature.

Getting Started

The photo you choose to inspire your water, mountain, or winter scene can be as humble as a vacation snapshot or as majestic as a professional photographer's greatest ocean sunset. The photos here reflect that diversity: Natalie's view of the lake from her summer cabin (right) or Nancy's backyard in snow (bottom right) are simple compared with the two more glamorous postcards of lakes in Kentucky (below).

Choosing Fabrics

Even more important than your photo are the fabrics that you choose. Having the right fabrics for water, sky, mountains, or snow can make the humblest scene come alive.

Sky and Water Fabrics

Visit a nearby fabric store. Look at the batiks and, if your store has them, the hand-dyed fabrics. Now think about the sky. Don't get hung up on blue sky and white puffy clouds. Consider the way the sky appears at sunrise, at sunset, before a storm, after a storm, in the heat of the summer, in the cool of fall, in the dreary dregs of winter. These images should suggest a rainbow of colors: gray, purple, yellow, blue, and peach.

The same is true of water, which often reflects what is happening in the sky. If the sky is blue, the water may be as well. But more often, the water has as many colors as the sky.

If you've chosen a lake or ocean scene, sky and water will dominate your quilt. Since they take up so much space, make that space dramatic. Let your imagination play with the wonderful variety of batiks and hand-dyed fabrics that are available to you these days. If your local store doesn't carry them, check out Internet sources or attend regional or national quilt shows where fabric vendors present their wares. (See "Resources" on page 143.)

Mountain Fabrics

Mountain fabrics can be mysterious. Until you actually cut them out and place them on a background fabric, you won't know whether they will work or not. Never choose a solid. A mountain range needs a variety of hues or shades, vertically aligned. Batiks and hand-dyes make great mountain ranges because of their abstract movement of color and hue. Mountains can be gray, tan, purple, or any color—it all depends on the weather in your

scene. And remember, you can enhance shading on your mountain range by using fabric markers or paint.

Snow Fabrics

This fabric doesn't necessarily have to be white. You might need gray, light blue, pale purple, or even teal, depending on your overall scene. Again, never choose a solid. Make sure your snow has some texture or variety of hue. Study winter scenes carefully. Notice how important shadows, ridges, and drifts are and how their movements are horizontal. You can enhance the sense of snowdrifts and shadows with fabric paint and markers, but always start with the most accurate fabric you can find.

Accent Fabrics

For added interest, water, mountain, and snow scenes need shrubs, trees, ground cover, and perhaps some flowers. You learned how to make these in earlier chapters. Messy- or fussy-cut your greenery, depending on what scale you need your accent elements to be.

Use a dark green fabric for trees, shrubs, or ground cover.

Snow

Sky

Water and Sky

Mountains

Creating a Horizon Line in Water Scenes

If you have selected effective fabrics, creating a water/sky scene with a horizon line (or strip) is easy.

 See "Cutting and Gluing" on page 20 for more information.

Choosing Fabric

First, choose a compatible water/sky combination. A stormy sea with a calm sky makes no sense. Look for matching colors and moods. Sometimes, the only difference between water and sky is horizontal wave markings on the water fabric. In that case, perhaps the same piece of fabric can be used for both water and sky.

The two water/sky combinations shown at right are actually one fabric. The stormy view is the right side of the fabric *(Photo A)*, and the calm view is the wrong side *(Photo B)*.

Note from Natalie: Mickey Lawler, who owns Skydyes, created the fabric in these photos. Mickey hand-paints 100%-cotton broadcloth with textile inks, some of which are pearlescent. No two fabrics are exactly alike. She sells at quilt shows and through direct mail. (See "Resources" on page 143.) Her work is especially useful to landscape quilters, since her scenic fabrics give you a running start on your project.

You will probably want to use two different fabrics for your scene: one for water and another for sky. Decide which should be dominant, the water or the sky. Then cut the two fabrics the same width. Make the dominant fabric approximately two-thirds of the design and the other one-third. Overlap the two fabrics and glue them together *(Photo C)*.

- To make the horizon line itself, pick a fabric that has some vertical texture—that is, it has directional movement along the lengthwise grain of the fabric. Make sure it makes sense with your scene. That is, if your scene is dark and stormy, pick a dark and stormy mountain or hill range. If it's golden and sunny, choose a lighter fabric. Natalie and Nancy chose a gray muted fabric for the blue/gray scene and a much darker, more dramatic hand-dye for the stormy scene. The width of your horizon piece depends on the distance from the front of your scene to the horizon. If you are fairly close, it will be thicker. If far away, it will be much narrower.

- Messy-cut the top of the horizon line to create the illusion of distant mountains or hills. The bottom should be completely straight. Place it either higher or lower than the center of your background fabric. If you place it exactly in the middle of your water and sky fabric, you create an uninteresting symmetry. For instructions on how to make dramatic mountains, see "Creating *Tiffany Mountains*" on page 118.

Showcase of Water Scenes

Golden Morning **by Natalie Sewell (39" x 35")**

few years ago, Natalie bought several pieces of Mickey Lawler's Skydye fabrics without having any idea what she would do with them. She hung them on her design wall for a while. Finally, it occurred to her that the yellow/gold/green/peachy fabric looked like water and shoreline all in one and the other piece looked like sky. She created trees, rocks, and shoreline and cut a horizon line from a piece of green fabric that had a tiny dot pattern with some vertical lines.

On the right side of the horizon line, Natalie capped the top of the green hill with tulle (bridal veil) to lighten it. The border was a happy accident; she found a piece of fabric that changed shades gradually, and when she auditioned the fabric for a border, it made the gold tones in the scene glow. One of the advantages of having a big stash is uncovering fabric finds like this one.

Lake Superior **by Natalie Sewell (38" x 44")**

$\mathcal{N}$atalie calls *Lake Superior* one of the simplest quilts she's never made. Not wanting to interfere with the dramatic effects of her Skydye fabrics, she added only three birch tree trunks and some messy-cut shrubs and ground cover. She machine-embroidered the tree branches and tall grasses after the quilt top was finished, but before it was quilted. (See machine-embroidery techniques, page 128.) Natalie created a sense of distance by making the horizon line of cliffs very narrow. She used fabric paint to enhance the tree trunks and bordered the piece with a very simple commercial batik.

Irises at the Pond **by Nancy Zieman (30" x 37")**

Natalie gave Nancy the background fabric for this quilt: a yard of Mickey Lawler's Skydye print. Nancy loves purple, so she was excited about planning a quilt around this fabric.

Nancy began by pinning the background piece to a wall in her office, trying to decide if it should be sky, water, or mountains. For months, she thought the quilt was going to be a mountain scene.

Inspiration came at a meeting at Nancy's local hospital. In the meeting room hung a large photo of Siberian irises growing along the edge of a pond.

Nancy had a difficult time concentrating on the meeting because she was so intent on memorizing the photo. During a break she sketched the scene and made notes.

Using techniques described in Chapter 3 (starting on page 45), Nancy created what is essentially a flower garden quilt on a water background. Notice that there is no horizon line for this body of water—the scene's background is all water.

Nancy made the distant portion of the pond by adding lily pads in the upper left-hand corner. These lily pads are paler and lighter to create a sense of distance in contrast to the brighter, more distinct lily pads in the foreground.

Creating *Once in a Purple Moon*

A piece of purple hand-dyed fabric
and a view from her door inspired
Nancy to make this quilt.

***Once in a Purple Moon* by Nancy Zieman (31" x 40")**

$\mathcal{W}$ith no particular project in mind, Nancy purchased a yard of hand-dyed purple fabric. Since she gravitates toward jewel tones, she found this fabric irresistible.

One evening, months later, she looked across the road at her neighbor's tree highlighted by a full moon and a purple sky and then remembered the purple fabric.

The tree, the moon, and the sky were the only portions of that scene that showed up in Nancy's landscape quilt. The mountains, the shoreline, and the lake of the quilt don't exist in the original scene. They came from Nancy's imagination.

She let the background fabric dictate her color choices. She envisioned teal and mauve moonlit mountains, a jade lake, dark green lakeshore, and even purple leaves.

The moon, which Nancy placed over the brightest part of the hand-dyed fabric, is made from gray batik, not a white fabric, as it might appear. The shoreline shrubs, grasses and extra tree branches aren't fabric at all but machine embroidery (see the detail photo below). (See Chapter 7, page 128, for more information on using machine embroidery.)

Quick Bias Borders

Rather than adding a pieced border, Nancy used black Quick Bias to create a stained-glass effect. This bias border was added after machine-stitching the cutout pieces to the background and squaring up the quilt top. Here are the steps to follow for making a Quick Bias border like this one:

- Determine the placement of the Quick Bias tape. Measure and accurately mark lines for placement.
- Remove the paper backing from the Quick Bias. (See Chapter 1, page 17, for Quick Bias details.)
- Press the Quick Bias in place, taking special precautions to apply the tape as straight as possible. If the tape wavers in a crooked line, press it with an iron to warm and soften the fusible web; then reposition.
- Permanently stitch the Quick Bias tape to the quilt top with a 4.0 double needle or straight-stitch on each side of the tape.

Note from Nancy: A double needle can be used on any sewing machine where the needle threads from front to back, which is practically every model ever made. The needle has one shank with two needles. The number of the double needle—in this instance 4.0—refers to the distance in millimeters between the two needles.

- Place two spools of thread on the thread spindle; or wind two bobbins and use them on the thread spindle. Treat the threads as one until threading the needles.
- The bobbin thread handles both needles and both threads and creates a stitch on the underside that resembles a zigzag. The topstitching is perfectly straight since both rows are stitched simultaneously.

This quilt now hangs in Nancy's sister and brother-in-law's Frank Lloyd Wright-style house, which is just the right setting for this contemporary landscape quilt.

You can purchase premade ¼"-wide Quick Bias in colors. The back of the bias is bonded with paper-backed fusible web. Simply remove the paper backing and press it in place; then secure with machine stitching.

Creating *Tiffany Mountains*

Inspiration for this quilt came from a postcard that Nancy purchased at the Metropolitan Museum of Art in New York City. She pinned the postcard to her bulletin board, where it hung for months. When she bought that card, she had never met Natalie and had no idea that the card would not only inspire her first landscape quilt, but that she would become totally immersed in this form of quilting.

Tiffany Mountains by Nancy Zieman (47" x 36")

Creating Sky and Water

• Overlap and glue two-thirds of sky to one-third of water *(Photo A)*. Please note that the fabric is not identical to the two prints used in the original scene. The scene was made years ago, and the original fabric is no longer available.

B

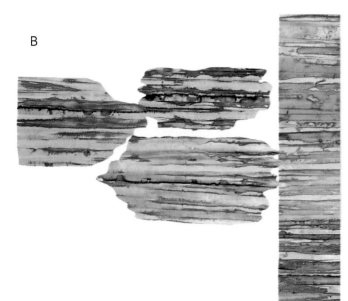

- The yellow in the sky spreads over the entire width of the fabric. To create one light source, thus focusing the sunset in one spot, Nancy covered the majority of the yellow by cutting gray or beige sections from the fabric and gluing them over the yellow areas *(Photos B and C).*

Note from Nancy: When using commercially dyed fabrics for sky and water, you'll frequently find a repeat of the light areas. As you cover the unneeded light spots with large sections of unused background fabric, be careful that the overlaid sections blend into the background.

Creating Mountain Shapes

- Choose batik or multicolored fabrics for mountain shapes to give the appearance of hills and valleys. (See "Choosing Fabrics," page 109.)
- To create realistic mountain shapes, cut concave indentations. The more pitched the indentations, the more majestic the mountains. A more gradual pitch creates low-lying mountains or hills *(Photo D).*
- To create the appearance of a range of foreground mountains, add small peaks cut from darker batik fabrics. Or add peaks of tulle (bridal veil) to make shadows or a hint of snow *(Photo E).*

Note from Nancy: Since this was my first landscape quilt, I can see areas that I would do differently today. For example, I made lollipop-shaped background shrubbery then; today, I would messy-cut that shrubbery. I look at it as part of the learning curve.

C

D

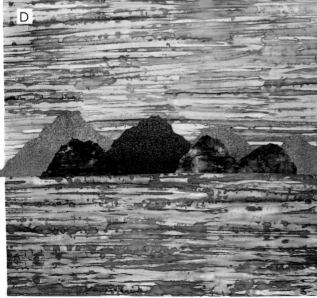

E

Creating a
Winter Scene

Winter scenes can be dramatic and beautiful and, because of their limited color range, stunning studies in contrast. To help you become comfortable working with these stark contrasting scenes, follow the step-by-step instructions that begin on the next page.

Winter Trees by Natalie Sewell (36" x 26")

Creating *Winter Trees*

Because there is little foliage in the winter, making a winter landscape quilt can be a good beginning project.

Choosing Fabrics

- Select two background fabrics for this quilt: sky and snow. A gray, cloudy sky conveys winter effectively. Choose a hand-dyed fabric with mottled texture to create the effect of clouds. For snow, try a stark white fabric rather than a cream one and, if possible, a fabric with a little texture to it to create the effect of drifts and shadows. If you can't find one with texture, you can add texture with a light gray fabric marker.
- Choose a dark or black tree fabric. Black will show up best against the gray background. *Winter Trees* has only one tree fabric for all seven trees, but you may want to choose several different dark fabrics for your trees.
- Choose a gold fabric for the leaves. In the absence of a gold leaf fabric, you can always cut out tiny leaves from any gold fabric.

Creating the Background

 See "Cutting and Gluing" on page 20 before continuing.

A

- Messy-cut the top of the snow fabric, creating a small gentle hill. The uneven terrain creates interest in this simple scene. Position and glue it a third of the way up from the bottom of the gray sky fabric *(Photo A)*.

Sky

Snow

Tree

Leaves

122

Adding the Trees

- Cut half a dozen or so trees from your dark tree fabric. Vary the trunk widths to make them more interesting. Starting with the tree farthest back, stagger their positions in the snow *(Photo B)*.
- Cut branches from skinny strips of tree fabric. Make the strips skinnier the farther they are from the tree trunk. Make the tiniest branches at the tips with machine embroidery or a black fabric marker. (See "Machine-Embroidery Techniques" on page 128.)

Note from Nancy: Initially, my trees lacked a realistic look, and I couldn't pinpoint what was wrong. Natalie took one look at the in-progress design, removed the curved branches, and repositioned them with branches that had an "elbow" or a bend. This simple design tip can add the realistic touch to any landscape scene.

Embellishing the Trees

- Cut elongated, irregular triangles of white snow fabric to nestle between the branches and the trunks of the trees. Add taller triangles to the base of the tree trunks *(Photos C and D)*.
- Cut out tiny gold leaves and glue them to some of the branches of the trees *(Photos C and D)*. Cluster them randomly.
- Machine-embroider weeds and grasses in the snowy foreground of your scene and add additional branches to the trees *(Photo E)*. (See "Machine-Embroidery Techniques" on page 128.)

See "Machine-Stitching the Quilt Top" on page 21 for more information.

See "Squaring Up the Quilt Top" on page 23 for more information.

B

C

D

E

***Winter Trees* by Natalie Sewell (36" x 26")**

Winter in the Park by Natalie Sewell (46" x 21")

One snowy afternoon—the perfect weather for quilting—Natalie decided to try to capture the barren look of the trees outside her window. A postcard of a snow-covered Central Park proved a great help (see below).

After she had glued down the two biggest trees and the lamp, she felt no need to stick with her photo.

In her stash, Natalie found a piece of dark gray fabric that grew lighter in the middle and then faded back to dark. This became her background fabric. The snow is a piece of white muslin with shadows of darker fabric here and there and a few bits of grass fabric scattered about.

Notice that like the trees in *Two Dogwoods* (see page 88), these trees grow paler as they recede into the distance. Starting as far away as possible with the palest of trees, Natalie gradually added darker and darker trees to the foreground, making the foremost tree jet black. That is an effective way to create depth in a landscape scene.

Winter in the Park is owned by Judith Faulkner and hangs in the employee commons of her company, Epic Systems Corporation, in Madison, Wisconsin.

7

Finishing Touches

There is more to finishing a landscape quilt than attaching the binding. Extra touches make a significant difference in how the quilt looks and hangs on your wall.

Therefore, this chapter covers not only binding, but also the extra finishing touches that make your quilt special. We'll discuss embellishing your landscape quilt with machine embroidery, as well as hand embroidery with silk ribbon and floss. We'll describe how to make three-dimensional leaves and offer techniques for free-motion quilting, stippling, making a sleeve, and labeling your quilt. We'll show you how to block your quilt so that it hangs flat on the wall, and, finally, we'll share our secrets for fixing quilts that don't turn out quite right.

September by Natalie Sewell
(51" x 48")

127

Embellishing the Landscape

You can add more decorative elements to your landscape quilt with machine embroidery, silk ribbon embroidery, and cotton floss embroidery. Choose the technique you like best or combine a little of each.

Machine Embroidery

Machine embroidery is effective for making tiny branches and twigs or distant trees that are too small and delicate to cut from fabric. You can also use it to create grasses, weeds, and foliage *(Photos A and B)*. Add machine embroidery after you have finished machine-stitching all your cutout pieces in place and before you layer your quilt.

To set up your sewing machine for machine embroidery, refer to page 21. Follow all the same guidelines, except use a machine embroidery needle and machine embroidery thread instead of monofilament thread.

Thread Choices

There are two kinds of thread for machine embroidery: rayon and cotton. Rayon (40 weight) creates a lustrous sheen. Cotton (30 weight) has a matte finish and blends perfectly with cotton fabrics.

Machine-Embroidery Techniques

- Using a fine-point mechanical pencil, lightly sketch your embroidery design onto the background fabric.
- Place the fabric under the presser foot.
- Lower the feed dogs and attach a darning foot.
- Keep the fabric taut by holding the fabric while wearing rubber fingers. Or place a hoop, such as the Quilt Sew Easy™, on top of the fabric. Place your hands lightly on the sides of the hoop and move the hoop under the needle.
- Hold the top thread taut. Stitch in place two to four stitches. Clip the thread tail.

Note from Natalie: Some quilters pull the bobbin thread to the top of the quilt. Since a wall hanging involves a great deal of machine stitching, but gets little heavy use and no machine washing, I usually just stitch in place.

- Stitch, using a medium fast speed, while moving the fabric left to right, front to back, or diagonally, following the pencil outline *(Photo C)*.
- When you are finished embroidering an area, sew two to three stitches in place. Clip the top thread.

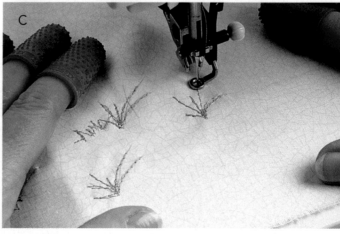

D

Hand Embroidering with Silk Ribbon

The forest floor in Natalie's quilt *September* (pages 126–127 and 130) features grasses made from silk ribbon stitches, an easy touch that adds dimension to your quilt *(Photo D)*.

Silk Ribbon Selection

Use 4-mm-wide silk ribbon. Select four to six colors within one color family. For example, if you are making grasses or foliage, choose numerous shades of green *(Photo E)*.

Silk Ribbon Embroidery Techniques

- Cut a length of silk ribbon approximately 14" to 16" long. (Longer lengths often fray or shred.) Cut an end on the diagonal and insert it through the eye of a silk ribbon embroidery or crewel needle *(Diagram A)*.
- To secure the ribbon end and to prevent raveling, insert the needle point ¼" from the end of the ribbon. Pull the opposite end of the ribbon, bringing the end closer to the needle eye. Slip the ribbon end over the needle eye, cinching the ribbon end against the needle *(Diagram B)*.
- Tie a soft knot on the opposite end of the ribbon by folding the ribbon ¼" from the end and inserting the needle through the folded section *(Diagram C)*. Gently pull the ribbon through the end stitch, forming the soft knot.
- To make the **in-and-out stitch** used for grasses, bring the ribbon up through the fabric. Fluff and straighten the ribbon with the right side of the needle. Insert the needle at the end point. Bring it out again at the top of the next piece of grass. Pull the ribbon through the fabric *(Diagram D)*.

E

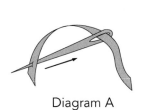

Diagram A

Diagram B

Diagram C

Diagram D

Note from Natalie: Instead of silk ribbon, consider using cotton embroidery floss. I highlighted the grass area of *Kentucky Dogwoods* with several shades of green floss. Use at least six strands of floss to enhance the graphic impact on your quilt.

Showcase of Embellished Quilts

September **by Natalie Sewell (51" x 48")**

September illustrates several of the finishing techniques outlined in this chapter. It features three-dimensional leaves on the golden tree as well as four colors of silk ribbon grasses and hand-appliquéd leaves scattered on the ground.

The several shades of green grasses add depth to the scene, and the sheen of the silk gives a dewy luster. Natalie liked the effect of the silk ribbon enough to use it again and again in woodland foreground scenes.

September won first prize in Pictorial Quilts at the American Quilter's Society Show in Paducah, Kentucky, in 1996.

The Clothesline by Natalie Sewell (60" x 48")

ike many of Natalie's works, this playful quilt was inspired by a woodland scene. However, in this quilt, Natalie hand-appliquéd a clothesline hung with clothes and linens blowing in the breeze in the foreground to give the quilt a touch of whimsy. The line is a piece of silk yarn attached only at the ends. The clothes, the towels, and the sheet are scraps of cotton fabrics. "The challenge was getting them to look like they were wind tossed," says Natalie. "You can imagine how many pieces of fabric I auditioned before I settled on the final few."

Natalie chose to appliqué these particular pieces by hand so that she could control how windblown they appeared. A machine stitch would have flattened them and broken the illusion. She added the hand-appliquéd details after she machine-stitched the quilt top and added the borders—just before she layered the quilt.

Layering Your Quilt

When the top of your landscape quilt is complete, it's time to add the backing and the batting.

- Choose a backing fabric that fits the mood of your scene. It does not need to be one of the fabrics used in the quilt, but it should harmonize with the quilt top. For example, a spring floral fabric would be a good choice for a scene featuring tulips but a poor choice for a fall tree scene.

Note from Natalie: When I began making landscape quilts, I was inexperienced at free-motion stitching, and my stitches were very uneven. Until I got better, I often chose busier prints for backings to hide my uneven stitches.

- Use a lightweight batting (for example, Pellon Polyester Fleece™. See page 15 for a description of the fleece).
- Place the backing wrong side up on a flat surface, such as a table; if the quilt is large, you may prefer to use the floor. Secure the backing to the surface with masking tape *(Diagram A)*. Give the corners a little tug, stretching them gently so that the backing is completely smooth. This helps eliminate puckers as you machine-quilt.
- Place the batting on top of the backing and smooth it out with your hands. Then place the quilt top right side up on the batting *(Diagram B)*.
- Pin the layers of the quilt together with Quilter's Safety Pins or Curved Basting Pins, spacing pins about 3" (7.5 cm) apart (photo below). Use your fist as a measuring guide in spacing the pins *(Diagram C)*. This adequately secures the layers yet won't interfere with the machine quilting.

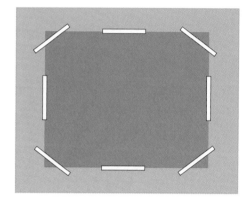

Diagram A

Diagram B

Diagram C

Setting Up Your Machine and Workstation

To quilt effectively, you will need an extended work area that supports the weight of your quilt. This space should be well lit. Here are several workstation options to make the final quilting process relaxing, while producing professional results.

- Your sewing machine should be set in a cabinet or on a tabletop that has enough of an extension to create a flat work surface. Here are three examples:
  - In Nancy's office sewing room, she has added a tabletop extension and a sewing light to the machine *(Photo A)*.
  - Natalie's studio sewing station features a sewing machine and cabinet *(Photo B)*.
  - Nancy's sewing room at home has another sewing machine with the cabinet option *(Photo C)*.
- Adjust your chair height so that your elbows are even with the tabletop, without causing you to tense your shoulders. Select an office or sewing chair with a padded seat and a back that has an adjustable height *(Photo D)*.
- Should you notice aches and pains in your neck or back while sewing, stop and rest for a while.

Note from Natalie: When I began machine quilting, my neck would ache after only an hour of work. When I raised my chair height several inches so that I could relax my shoulders, I had no more neck pain, even after hours of quilting. The proper chair height is as important as the proper machine setting for quilting. Also, keep several quilts going at once at different stages so that you can change your tasks often.

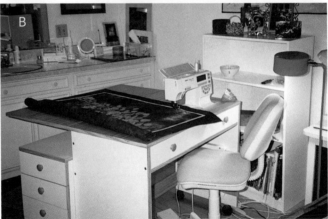

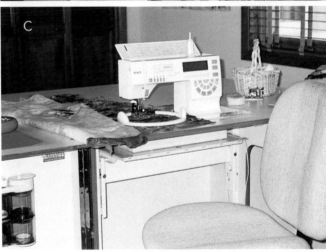

D

Free-Motion Stitching

Use free-motion sewing machine stitching to secure the three layers of your quilt together. This stitching is what gives your quilt its texture and personality. Although free-motion quilting is time-consuming, it can also be enjoyable and relaxing.

In **free-motion stitching,** you use the stitching to trace your fabric's design. When you see leaves, you stitch the leaves; when you see ground cover, you stitch its outlines. You follow the lines of tree trunks up and down. You trace the outlines of flowers. You let the fabric speak to you and allow the scene's design to suggest stitching patterns.

When you stitch an area of your quilt that has no printed pattern, such as sky or borders, you will make up your own pattern of little "squibbles" that quilters call **stippling.** Each quilter has her own style. Stippling patterns can be tiny with no lines crossing others, or they can be larger and more relaxed. As you become more experienced, you will develop your own quilting style.

A

Note from Natalie: My stippling style for borders is in the form of puzzle pieces; Nancy's is leaves. Our styles seemed to evolve on their own without any conscious decision on our parts.

The following guidelines apply to both free-motion stitching and stippling.
- Lower the feed dogs and attach a darning foot.
- If your quilt is much larger than your worktable, roll the quilt toward the center from each short end. Secure the rolled sections with pins or bicycle clips *(Diagram)*.
- Begin stitching at the center and work out toward the borders. Complete the entire landscape scene before you begin the borders.
- Wear rubber fingers or use a Quilt Sew Easy™ hoop to stabilize the fabric *(Photo A)*.
- Sew at a medium to fast speed and move the fabric slowly.
- Remove the safety pins as you come to them.
- Reroll the fabric as you complete stitching in one area.
- The same stitching intensity should extend over the entire quilt surface. If you've stitched heavily and finely in the center of the quilt, do the same in the rest of the scene and in the border. If your quilt is unevenly stitched, the finished landscape will not be flat or square. If your border is not stitched as heavily as the body of the quilt, it will pucker and looked ruffled.
- Experiment with various stitching options. Water can be represented by horizontal stitching lines or by fine stippling.

Diagram

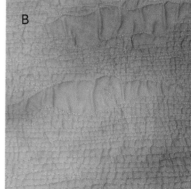

B

C

D

You may want to stitch your sky horizontally, leaving small areas unstitched to resemble clouds *(Photo B)*.
- Small areas that are not stitched will appear to come forward in the design. Tree trunks and flowers that are outline-stitched will look three-dimensional *(Photos C and D)*.

Stitching the Borders

Use straight stitching to create a mat around the quilted scene.
Then add stippling to the remaining border area, and your quilt is nearly complete.

Quilted Borders

Stitch in-the-ditch (in the seam line) between the border and your scene to create a mat line. This easy step gives a finished look to your landscape quilt.

- Raise the feed dogs and engage the dual feed, if applicable to your sewing machine.
- Attach the regular presser foot.
- Use the same needle-and-thread combination as you did for free-motion stitching the body of your quilt.
- Stitch in-the-ditch, sewing along the seam between the quilt scene and the border. This stabilizes the quilt and defines one edge of a simulated mat *(Diagram A)*.
- Form the second edge of the mat by stitching in the border ½" or a presser-foot width away from the first stitching. Stitch a second time over the same area for reinforcement and emphasis *(Diagram B)*.

Stippling Options

Adjust the machine for free-motion stitching and stipple the border area. Below are photos of some mat and stippling options for creating effective borders.

Note from Natalie: Remember to quilt the borders of your landscape as intensively as other areas of the quilt. If you don't, the borders will ripple and the quilt may not hang flat on the wall.

Diagram A

Diagram B

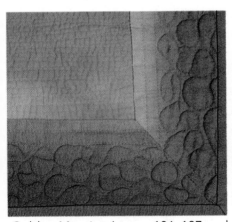

Golden Morning (pages 106–107 and 111) features a double inner border.

In *It Could Be October* (page 141), both inner and outer borders are stippled with a leaf design.

For *Wisteria* (pages 74–75 and 76–77), the wide inner border features a straight stitching treatment. Note that the inner border has fabric shapes overlapped onto it.

Binding Your Quilt

Binding adds a finishing touch to the edges of your quilt. Follow these instructions to make a ½" double-fold French binding.

- Cut straight-grain binding strips 3" wide. Join the strips as needed to have sufficient length for all four sides of the quilt. Joining strips on the bias (by joining with a diagonal seam) reduces bulk when the binding is folded to the wrong side.
- Cut the end of the strip at a 45° angle. Fold in ¼" at one short end of the binding. Fold the binding in half, with wrong sides together, meeting lengthwise edges and press *(Diagram A)*.
- Meet cut edges of the binding to the quilt top, beginning at the center of one edge of the quilt, with right sides together. Mark the quilt top ½" from each corner. Stitch the binding to the quilt top with a ½" seam, stopping stitching at the marked point *(Diagram B)*. Lock stitches by stitching in place or stitching in reverse.
- Fold the binding up at a 45° angle, aligning the cut edge of the binding with the cut edge of the quilt *(Diagram C)*.
- Fold the binding down, meeting the binding fold to the top edge of the quilt and the binding cut edges to the quilt side edges. Stitch a ½" seam on the side, starting at the marked point *(Diagram D)*. Repeat at the remaining corners.
- When the binding reaches the starting point again, overlap the binding and trim the excess.
- Fold and press the binding away from the quilt *(Diagram E)*.
- Fold the binding to the wrong side, covering the stitching line and tucking in the corners to form miters. Handstitch the folded edges of the binding to the quilt backing *(Diagram F)*.

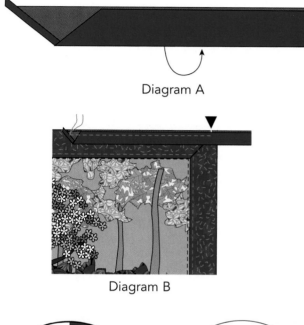

Diagram A

Diagram B

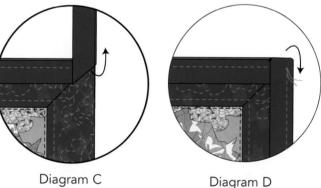

Diagram C

Diagram D

Diagram E

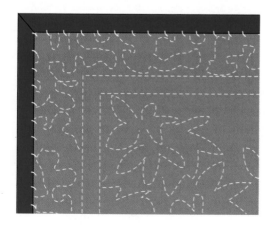

Diagram F

Adding a Hanging Sleeve

A hanging sleeve lets you display your quilt on a wall after it has been completed. The sleeve described below doesn't pinch the corners and becomes invisible on the wall.

- Cut an 8" strip of fabric from the backing fabric, cutting the strip 1" shorter than the width of the quilt.
- Turn under ¼" at both short ends of the strip and press *(Diagram A)*.
- Fold the strip in half, with right sides together, meeting the lengthwise edges. Stitch a ¼" seam along the lengthwise edge to form a tube *(Diagram B)*. Turn the tube right side out and press.
- Center the tube on the upper edge of the quilt, positioning it ½" from the top. Handstitch along the lower fold *(Diagram C)*.
- Fold back the sleeve ½" from the top fold; handstitch the sleeve to the quilt, catching only the first layer of fabric. The recessed stitching allows the quilt to hang parallel to the wall without buckling or pulling down the corners *(Diagram D)*.

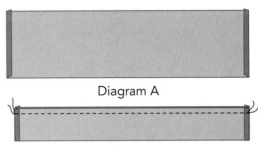

Diagram A

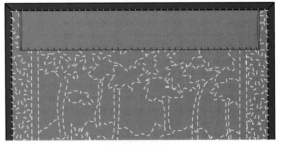

Diagram B

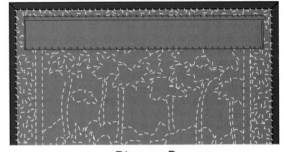

Diagram C

Diagram D

Trim Loose Threads and Edges

Give your finished landscape quilt a "haircut" to remove any edges of fabric that have become fringed, fuzzy, or whiskered. Machine appliquéing inevitably leaves frayed edges and loose threads, and now is the time to remove as many as you can. Place the quilt on your lap; using sharp embroidery scissors, hold the blades of the scissors parallel to the quilt top and trim stray threads and frayed fabric edges. After you've finished trimming the quilt top, turn the quilt over and clip any loose bobbin threads from the back.

Spring by Natalie Sewell (24" x 31") ▶

Natalie designed *Spring* for her first public TV appearance with Nancy. Nancy asked her to make the quilt no bigger than a large TV screen. At first Natalie thought this meant that PBS's technology was too primitive to film anything larger than a TV monitor. But Nancy explained that if the quilt were too large, it would scarcely leave room on camera for people, tools, and props.

"Making such a small landscape scene was a challenge," says Natalie. "I was used to taking all the room I needed." If you're a beginner, you may think that smaller is easier—but it isn't. "Unless you're lucky enough to be working with Nancy, give yourself plenty of room," Natalie advises.

Blocking

Blocking gives your quilt a finished look. No matter how careful your craftsmanship has been every step of the way, inevitably a corner of your quilt will curl a little or a section will buckle. Blocking your quilt on a vertical surface with plenty of hot steam will convince it to lie flat against the wall.

- Return your quilt to your vertical design wall. Pin it in place and pin flat any section that buckles or curls.
- Using a small damp hand towel, cover a section of the quilt.
- Press the quilt through the towel, using a hot iron. The process should provide plenty of steam.
- Move the damp towel to the next area of the quilt. Rewet the towel if necessary. Press.
- Pin the bottom corners flat and make sure the quilt is hanging as it should.
- Allow the quilt to dry overnight on the vertical surface.

Labeling Your Quilt

Your finished quilt deserves a label. There are many fancy ways to label a quilt, but here's a simple, quick option that provides the needed information and maintains the mood you created in your landscape quilt.

- Cut a rectangle, approximately 4" x 6", of light-colored fabric that coordinates with the backing fabric.
- Press under ¼" along all sides of the square.
- Cut out and glue a few motifs (such as you used on the quilt front) in one of the corners of your fabric square. For example, if your landscape quilt depicted irises, glue a few blossoms and leaves from some iris. Free-motion stitch the motifs to the label fabric.
- With a permanent marker, write your quilt's name, your name, and the date you completed the quilt on the label square (see photo at right). If you are submitting your quilt to a quilt show, add your address and phone number.
- Hand-appliqué your label to the lower left-hand corner of the quilt's backing.

Note from Natalie: In addition to making a label and sewing it to the backing, I write my initials on the back of the quilt with a permanent ink pen. I also write my initials on the front of the quilt, usually in the lower right-hand corner on a leaf, a blade of grass, or a tree trunk, where it won't be conspicuous.

Showcase

Pansies **by Natalie Sewell** ▶
(26" x 25")

This happy little quilt came from a sudden impulse to garden in February. Winters in Wisconsin are long, and Natalie couldn't wait until spring, so she planted a few pots with fabric.

◀***Dinosaur Times***
by James Peranteau
(35" x 28")

No one is too old or too young to make a landscape quilt. Natalie's grandson, James, age 10, made the dinosaur quilt shown at left. It is his fourth quilt.

Fixing Mistakes

*One of the nicest features of machine-appliquéd landscape quilts
is how forgiving they are. Long after you've decided that you've finished the quilt,
you can redesign it without anyone being the wiser.*

You can fix your mistakes as often as you like. When you've finished a patchwork quilt, you're finished unless you want to take the whole thing apart. But with landscape quilts, all you have to do is rip out a piece here and there or add a new layer wherever you want, and you can remedy your design. The following examples illustrate our point.

Golden Woods by Natalie Sewell (48" x 37")

Natalie wanted to create a quilt depicting a glorious sunrise. She purchased a lovely piece of yellow hand-dyed fabric that she hoped would convey dawn. But somehow the finished quilt, shown at right, wasn't right. The background controlled the foreground, and the yellow seemed too glaring. The duller foreground leaves appeared flat. Natalie let the quilt hang in her studio for three months and reassured herself that it was fine. She tried to ignore her misgivings.

Finally, she realized what the quilt needed— something really bright in the foreground to offset the brilliant background. What better than a little crimson maple tree? She also cooled down the ground cover by adding green shrubbery and a variety of green grasses (see large photo below).

It Could Be October by **Nancy Zieman**
(46" x 42")

One evening as Nancy was designing this quilt, her youngest son looked at the design wall and chirped, "It could be October." Just that quickly, the quilt had a name.

When Nancy finished *It Could be October* (shown at right), she was happy with the name but unsettled about the design. She hung the quilt in her office, only to look at it daily and think, "There's something wrong with this design."

One day, while talking on the phone and subconsciously analyzing the quilt, Nancy realized the background trees were not the right color. They should have had the same intensity as the background. It was time to fix these mistakes.

With a seam ripper, Nancy diligently picked out the stippling stitches that secured the background trees. "I saved this task for a televised football game, which kept my mind off the tedious process," she says. "After removing the trees, the quilt was less busy and more restful to my eye."

As a final brightening step, Nancy added touches of gold leaves. The process took less than thirty minutes. Nancy could not find actual gold leaves in a fabric print, so she cut simple shapes from a multishaded gold fabric, glued them to the scene, and stippled the leaves in place (see large photo below).

It Could be October is back in Nancy's office. "I still look at it daily," she says. "But now I like what I see!"

Index

Resources

Hand-Dyed Fabrics for Backgrounds

ARTFABRIK
Laura Wasilowski and
   Melody Johnson
324 Vincent Place
Elgin, IL 60123
Phone: (847) 931-7684
Web site: www.artfabrik.com
E-mail: artfab@suba.com or
   mrsmel@mc.net

Quilt Tapestry Studio
Wendy Richardson
8009 Florida Avenue North
Brooklyn Park, MN 55445
Phone: (763) 566-3339
E-mail: wendyRQTS@aol.com

Confetti Works
Sharon Luehring
The Stitcher's Crossing, Ltd.
6108 Mineral Point Road
Madison, WI 53705
Phone: (608) 232-1500
Fax: (608) 232-1750
E-mail:
info@stitcherscrossing.com

SKYDYES
Mickey Lawler
P.O. Box 370116
West Hartford, CT 06137-0116
Phone: (860) 232-1429
Fax: (860) 236-9117
Web site: www.skydyes.com
E-mail: fabrics@skydyes.com

Commercial Batiks

The commercial suppliers of batik fabrics listed below are
widely available through fabric and quilt shops; they do not
sell directly to the public. As a service to quilters, each company has a page on its Web site to help you locate retail stores
and mail-order sources that stock its fabrics or information
on how your local retail store can carry its fabrics.

Hoffman Fabrics
www.hoffmanfabrics.com

Bali Fabrications/Princess Mirah Design
www.balifab.com

Island Batik, Inc.
www.islandbatik.com

Natalie Sewell, a renowned landscape quilter whose works have won major prizes at numerous national competitions, has been quilting for 10 years. Her awards include two first-place prizes and one second-place prize at the American Quilter's Society Show in Paducah, Kentucky, as well as inclusion in Quilt San Diego's "Visions" show. Natalie lives in Madison, Wisconsin, with her husband, Richard.

Nancy Zieman, a national sewing authority, is the producer and host of Public TV's "Sewing With Nancy." In addition, Nancy is founder and president of Nancy's Notions, a sewing and quilting supply catalog, a designer of patterns, and an author of numerous sewing and quilting books. Nancy lives in Beaver Dam, Wisconsin, with her husband and business partner, Rich, and their two sons, Ted and Tom.

For a complete line of sewing notions, turn to,
Nancy's Notions Sewing Catalog:
• Nancy Zieman's catalog for quilting, sewing, and serging enthusiasts.
• More than 4,000 products, including books, notions, videos, fabrics, and supplies!
• Value prices with built-in discounts!
• 100% satisfaction guaranteed!

For your free *Nancy's Notions* Sewing Catalog, send your name and address to:
Nancy's Notions
P.O. Box 683
Dept. 2318
Beaver Dam, Wisconsin 53916
Or call (800) 833-0690.